THE BOOK OF
SHERINGHAM

'Twixt Sea and Pine

PETER BROOKS

HALSGROVE

First published in Great Britain in 2009
reprinted 2011

British Library Cataloguing-in-Publication Data
A CIP record for this title is available from the British Library

ISBN 978 1 84114 944 8

HALSGROVE
Halsgrove House,
Ryelands Business Park,
Bagley Road, Wellington, Somerset TA21 9PZ
Tel: 01823 653777   Fax: 01823 216796
email: sales@halsgrove.com

Part of the Halsgrove group of companies
Information on all Halsgrove titles is available at: www.halsgrove.com

Printed and bound in the UK by the MPG Books Group

Frontispiece photograph: *Tom Barnes Cooper,
coxswain of the lifeboat* Augusta *(1859–94) and of
the lifeboat* Henry Ramey *(1894–98)*

CONTENTS

View of Sheringham from Franklin's Hill, c.1900.

Acknowledgements

It would not have been possible to cover the range of topics contained in this book without the help of the following people, to whom I owe a great debt of gratitude. I sincerely hope that if I have omitted anyone they will accept my heartfelt apologies.

My thanks go to Des Barney for his memories of an older Sheringham; Richard Childs and Peter Bacon for football memories and putting names to team members; Peter Cox for answering questions nobody else could answer; Roy Craske (the son of Stanley) for help across a wide range of Sheringham topics, especially regarding the Methodist Church and those families who have contributed so much to the town's growth, culture and history; Brian Farrow for information on Sheringham's lifeboats; Robin Goodfellow for cricketing memories and informa-tion; Geoff Gowen for his enthusiastic help in tracing the history of how the railway came to Sheringham, with every good wish for the continuing success of the North Norfolk Railway; Charles Hall for providing a first-class photographic service, taking copies of the dozens of photographs generously and trustingly loaned to me by families living in Sheringham.; Mike Slipper for all things educational, and trusting that he will, in due course, write his own book, which, I am sure, will be a best seller among proud parents and grandparents alike; Lennie 'Teapot' West for giving up a sunny August after-noon to help me put names to fishermen and other characters; Keigh Zealand for information on the National Trust and Sheringham's 'gem', Sheringham Park and its glorious grounds.

The coat of arms of Sheringham Town Council.

Introduction

My wife Naomi and I came to Sheringham in 1963 and since then I have been an avid collector of anything relating to what is now our home town and richly deserving of its claim to be 'the premier resort on the North Norfolk coast'.

During the course of some 40 years I have been fortunate enough to have built up an extensive literary and photographic library of Sheringham life. Many items have come from collectors' and postcard fairs, car boot sales, antique shops, generous donors and other sources. In many instances the origin of individual items is unknown, and whilst every effort has been made to trace the copyright owners of all items used there have been occasions when this has not been possible. Again, my apologies if this has happened, and I hope anyone interested will contact me so that I can make sure it will not happen again.

Peter Brooks
Sheringham

Sheringham Town Clock, symbol of the town.

Above and below: *Beeston Priory.*

✦ CHAPTER 1 ✦

Early Days

In her book *A History of Norfolk*, author Susanna Wade Martins reminds us that Norfolk is a relatively isolated county bordered by sea, rivers, fens and heaths.

Today we take road networks, rail systems and air flights for granted, but life some 400,000 years ago must have been grim, especially when invading hordes arrived to pillage, rape and conquer. Mesolithic sites have been identified on Kelling Heath, as have Stone-Age settlements and enclosures at Roughton. Gold coins, found in 1940 on the beach between Sheringham and Weybourne, were thought to have been left by members of a Gaulish tribe who inhabited the area during the first century BC. An axe, spearheads and pottery discovered at Beeston Regis have been dated back to the ninth century BC. It is known that Angles, Saxons and Vikings regularly attacked and plundered this coast and that Romans were also here, leaving one of their pottery kilns at Upper Sheringham.

We know that the town's name derives from a Scandinavian tribe led by Scira; it is, in effect, 'the home of Scira's people'. The Domesday Book records a church at Upper Sheringham, then known as Silingham, later Siringham and then Schyringham in 1291.

Sheringham was on a pilgrimage route to Walsingham, and in order to relieve the pressure on the existing priory at Weybourne a new one was planned for, and built, in 1216 at Beeston Regis. This large addition soon fell into disrepute when the monks were accused of 'vicious, carnal and abominable living'. It was closed in 1539. Today the abbey ruins can be explored, and it is a sobering thought that in its heyday this religious building gave this small hamlet an importance beyond that of the larger village of Sheringham, a superiority it took many years to reclaim.

If our knowledge of everyday life in Norfolk is sparse, perhaps we should be grateful that Lower Sheringham is a relatively 'new' town, coming into prominence with the arrival of the railway on 16 June 1887. Prior to this it had been a small, inward-looking, parochial fishing village, its inhabitants highly suspicious of strangers.

With the arrival of 'civilisation' Sheringham was 'discovered' by a whole range of people – the rich and famous looking for a place to build a second home by the sea, people a bit down the social scale searching for a new holiday resort to visit, and developers who could see money to be made in building new estates and providing such basic amenities as reliable water and sewerage systems, gas and electricity supplies, new streets and an improved prome-

A somewhat indistinct view of Sheringham in 1889, with (top left) *Admiral Villa, the home of John and Elizabeth Craske, built in 1835, and a row of three cottages in which lived brothers John 'Big' Craske, Robert 'Dinghy' Craske and Christopher 'Cutty' Craske.*

A view of Sheringham in the 1880s.

nade, as well as opening new shops and providing entertainment centres and all the other prerequisites of a modern society.

For their part local fishermen, always eager to find new sources of income, could see a new market opening for their services – providing beach huts, deckchairs, windbreaks, boat trips, donkey rides and accommodation for those who may well enjoy a stay in a 'quaint' fisherman's cottage. For many fishermen this developed into letting their entire cottage to a family whilst they and their children spent the summer in the garden shed or outhouse with, of course, mother supplying all meals for the visitors.

Two stories tell it all. When a rather condescending visitor confronted the late Cromer fisherman 'Shrimp' Davies with the comment: 'Norfolk – backside of England', his pomposity was quickly deflated by Shrimp's simple but telling response: 'What, are you just passing through?'. Or the holidaymaker commenting on the simpleness of the fishermen only to be told: 'You save up for 50 weeks in every year so that you and your family can enjoy a holiday. You stay in a fisherman's cottage and have all your meals provided. We then rent you a beach hut, deckchairs and windbreaks and take you all for a sea trip. We take all the money you have worked hard to save in just two weeks. So who is the smartest?' Response was there none!

Much of what we know about our town comes from memories either passed down verbally within families or written down and then filed away out of sight.

With boys often leaving school when aged only 10 or 12 years to go and help their fishermen fathers or as cabin boys away from their home town, their memories, if they have recorded any, can sometimes be difficult to read because of faded paper and less than perfect spelling. In the mid-1800s the village of Lower Sheringham comprised groups of small cottages of brick and flint construction, the flint being taken directly off the beaches. Buckets and barrels, together with crab and lobster pots, would be scattered around in abundance, and lines strung across the narrow streets would be heavy with recently washed slops, ganseys and rough worsted stockings.

The main residential areas were in lower High Street, Cooperative Street and Wyndham Street, all with virtually no gardens or open spaces around them.

According to one source, the male inhabitants of Lower Sheringham fell into one of two categories; they were either devoutly religious or of a 'devil may care' attitude – 'Shanny' – a Norfolk dialect word meaning 'excited, wild or scatterbrained'. Over the years anyone born in Sheringham became known as a 'Shannock', but to be a true member of this categorical society their parents should have been born in the town and, preferably, their grandparents as well.

In 1635 local man Thomas Heath was murdered near Pretty Corner. His attacker was traced, sentenced and hanged on the gallows at Gibbet Corner at the crossroads where the road from Pretty Corner crosses the A148 Cromer to Holt 'top road' to Gresham and West Beckham.

In 1673 local inhabitants petitioned the Lord Lieutenant for guns and ammunition to help repel a

Sheringham High Street, c.1880.

feared invasion by the Dutch. They stressed the great danger in which they lived:

... for the houses stand very close together and all houses thatched with straw. In one hour's time the town may be burnt for we have nothing to resist them but one gun with a broken carriage and four muskets which we bought at our own cost and charges. Likewise we have no powder for the said gun nor muskets when we stand in need.

They went on to ask for four to five muskets and half a hundred pounds each of powder and bullets so that the town could defend itself against any Dutch privateer. It has been suggested that the gun at the top of Gun Street dates back to this time of concern. They were given six muskets plus powder and bullets on condition that these were used only for the defence of Sheringham Hythe. The Hearth Tax of 1684 revealed that Sheringham had 100 occupied properties and two unoccupied, only 14 of the former having the luxury of two hearths.

In the early 1700s Sheringham was still being referred to as a 'town', this time with three lordships. Cook Flower owned the principal one, while Nutley Hall belonged to Thomas Windham of Cromer and Beeston Priory Manor was in the ownership of William Windham of Felbrigg. Fishing was still the main occupation, with crabs and lobsters the primary catches. These were chiefly supplied to the London markets by vessels '... which take the catches from the boats while still at sea'. There was a reference to 'a very fine inn, much resorted to in the summer for the sake of eating lobsters in their highest perfection'. From the description given, the inn is clearly the old Coffee House (Two Lifeboats), but the reference to 30 or 40 fishing boats within a mile of the shore 'and fleets of 300 colliers and other large trading vessels passing so near that with the naked eye you may discover the men on board' does seem somewhat exaggerated.

In a brief reference to local fishermen, it is said that the view:

... is enlivened by the multitude of fishermen either drying their nets, repairing their tackle, landing their fish or securing their crab and lobsters in a fort of boxes fixed to the rocks which the sea fills at every tide.

The House of Industry, a polite name for a workhouse, was built in Upper Sheringham in 1805 to provide accommodation for 100 inmates, mostly aged and infirm people drawn in not only from Sheringham, but also from the parishes of Felbrigg, Gresham, East Beckham, Cromer, Runton, Aylmerton, Aldborough and Beeston Regis. It closed

Sheringham in the early 1900s, photographed from Franklin's Hill looking north-east across the town. Note the lack of development in Hooks Hill Road, Abbey Road and Norfolk Road. Beeston Hills are in the background.

when a new workhouse was built at West Beckham. It was known locally as 'Beckham Palace', and in 1963 only the old hospital wing remained, occupied by people either with no home to go to or who found they did not fit into the society of the time.

In the late 1880s Sheringham consisted mainly of one central street – High Street. Research by old friend and colleague Stanley Craske showed there were no houses until you came to the present Robin Hood Inn (then known as the Railway Tavern). The old Primitive Methodist Chapel was in Pratt's Yard behind the inn. The site of the present clock tower was occupied by the town's reservoir, to which people came with buckets and pans to carry water home. A regular visitor was the dustcart, which was filled up with water so it could spray the streets after a dry spell. One lady has recorded the smell in the streets after spraying as being 'most refreshing'.

As in 2009, there were cottages behind what is now Starling's shop, and the present Cooperative Street was known either as The Piggeries or simply as Pig Street, as it led to a pig farm at the lower end. There was, however, no access to Beeston Road.

The Beeston Road Methodist Chapel was on its present site, then a few cottages, then nothing until you came to the main Cromer Road. According to Stanley's notes: 'You could run round lower Sheringham in ten minutes.'

Prior to the arrival of the railway in Sheringham in June 1887 you either walked or hired a pony and trap to go to Cromer, or if you knew the time the post was delivered to Sheringham you went to Barcham's Post Office and waited until he called your name. The same applied to telegrams, brought here from Cromer by a postman on horseback.

Although life back in the 1800s was without all the modern facilities which today we take for granted, records seem to show a united, friendly, caring population, in which neighbour cared for neighbour. Highlights were the visiting entertainments, such as the dancing bear and the organ grinder with his hurdy-gurdy and monkey. Also remembered is the unnamed fishermen with his cartload of herrings calling out 'Longshore herrins, 20 (sometimes 30) a shillin', and the lamplighter with his long pole lighting the gas lamps at dusk and putting them out in the early morning.

When Zeppelin L4 dropped its incendiary bomb in Whitehall Yard one lady was told to go indoors immediately. 'Git you indoors, my dear. He's a Garman and he'll see your white apron!' The same lady also remembered being involved in her school's first stage play. She played a courtier in *Cinderella* and recalled dancing the Veleta with the Ugly Sisters and performing with a group of 'somewhat hefty' fairies. She has also recalled Gofather Pegg taking a group from her school for a short trip out to sea. On their return to the beach the children helped GoFather haul his boat to the top of the beach, during which they joined him in his famous song:

Look upon the wall, you'll see a great spider,
Glory be to his long legs,
Hobbledy,Wobbledy, hit him on the nobbledy,
Then you'll see no more cobwebs.

Many of the streets and roads in Sheringham were once known by completely different names: Augusta Street was formerly known as Drift Lane; Beach Road was formerly known as North East Street, a name once also used for Wyndham Street; the lower part of Beeston Road, between Cliff Road and Avenue South,

Sheringham from the air.

was known as Paper Mill Road; Church Street, prior to 1838, was known as Upper Town Road; Coalyard Plain was situated to the rear of the Crown Inn and included the Emery family's boatbuilding two-storey workshop. At the time of writing it is known as Lifeboat Plain; Cox's Yard was to the rear of the present amusement arcade at the northern end of the present High Street; Gun Street was previously known as either Crown Road, Lob Lane or Lobster Lane. As late as 1963 tenants of the cottages had to cross the narrow street to use their toilets on the opposite side.

High Street has been known variously as The Street (1861), with its lower part, towards the promenade, being known as Cliff Street. It could also have been known as North Street; Morris Street was formerly known as Fisherman's Street.

There is some dispute about Pockthorpe; it could have been either Weston Terrace and its immediate area or the area of land from the rear of Barford Road to the area of common known as Back Common, with the railway bridge and line marking its southern boundary.

Pratt's Yard is now the site of the Post Office sorting depot behind the Robin Hood Inn. The latter was known as the First and Last inn c.l871 and as the Railway Tavern in 1881.

Pump Yard was an alternative name for Cox's Yard (see above); Slippers Loke connects High Street with Driftway via Morris Street; Tantivy Loke is the name given to the small alleyway (loke) behind the cottages in Gun Street; Tantivy Square was the name given to the car park area to the west of the Crown Inn. It has also been known as Woodhouse Yard and, more recently, as Chequers car park; Wyndham Street has been known variously as North East Street (1861) and Lombard Street (1871).

A Fair Do

In August 1929 Canon Upcher, then living at St Andrew's in St Joseph's Road, appears to have led a group of residents living in the area comprising The Rise, Heath Road, Cremer's Drift, St Joseph's Road, Cromer Road (part) and Common Lane who objected to a proposal by Mr 'Marlborough' Pegg to let some

A fine view of Sheringham.
(PHOTOGRAPH BY DEREK EDWARDS, COURTESY OF NORFOLK MUSEUM SERVICE)

land he owned in Heath Road for the purpose of setting up a fair.

When the Urban District Council said they had no powers to prevent the land being used for this purpose, the objectors asked Messrs Hansells, Hales & Bridgwater to act on their behalf. They were successful in obtaining an injunction preventing Mr Pegg, in perpetuity, from letting or using the land for the purpose of a fair. In a letter dated 30 November 1929 the solicitors outlined the action they had taken, including visits to London, consulting judges and preparing all the necessary and intricate legal documents.

Their representatives had also contacted Mr Pegg and Mr Kenneth Gray, the owner of the fair.

Mr. Pegg had agreed to accept the injunction and to pay £65 toward the plaintiffs' costs. Mr. Gray, however, had told the solicitors' representative that he was coming, 'and was going to make as much noise as possible'.

The solicitors stated that because of all the intricate work involved, the costs 'are somewhat heavy', amounting to £121.8s.9d., which, after deducting Mr Pegg's contribution, left the objectors to pay, collectively, the balance of £56.8s.9d. It is not known whether or not the fair was ever held.

It is interesting to note that at the time of this action the property known as St Andrew's was the last in St Joseph's Road, with fields beyond which could provide direct access to Beeston Common.

CHAPTER 2

Front Line Town

There is an old couplet that has a great deal of significance for Sheringham, situated as it is in the centre of the North Norfolk coast, with deep water close offshore:

He who would old England win
Must at Weybourne Hope begin.

For hundreds of years successive governments have considered this stretch of coastline to be a prime potential invasion area.

When, in 1588, the Spanish Armada threatened to invade us, the access to beaches was blocked, cliffs were fashioned to defined slopes and trenches were dug at strategic places along the cliff tops.

Rumours of a threatened invasion by the French in 1803 sparked further precautions, including the imposition of a scorched-earth policy should the enemy land. Only when it was realised that what had been thought to be an invasion fleet was, in fact, a convoy of merchant ships, was the policy cancelled. When a similar crisis arose during 1814/15 troops were stationed all along this stretch of coastline.

Early in the First World War Sheringham really did hit the national newspaper headlines. On 19 January 1915 two Zeppelins, under the overall command of Fregattenkapitän Peter Strasser, chief of the German Naval Airship Division, crossed the Norfolk coast at Bacton. Zeppelin L3 turned toward Great Yarmouth, whilst L4 turned west and headed, so its Commander, Kapitänleutnant Magnus Count von Platen Hallermand, thought, for the Humber estuary. When over Sheringham he thought he was over his target and dropped two incendiary bombs. One fell on waste land and did not explode. The second fell on a cottage in Whitehall Yard off Wyndham Street. After passing through the roof, bedroom ceiling and floor and kitchen ceiling it landed in a bucket, slightly injuring a young girl visiting the Smith family.

Sheringham Civil Defence members. Left to right, back row: *Ernie Abbs, Jack Horne, Joe Hall, Harry Barney, Frank Pyke, Ernest Stibbons, Jimmy Kemp, ? Piercy, Gordon Evatt, ?; second row: E. Blythe, Stanley Clipperton, E. Kimm, ?, F. Willeard, Sgt E. Turner, Jack Forsdick, Ted Stolworthy, W. Shepherd, ? Ash, Edwin Rose; front row: F. Cleall, Mrs Brian Smith, Mrs Jenkinson, ?, ?, Mrs Kilgour Baker, S.E. Day, Reg Randall, ?, ?, Mrs S.E. Day, ?, Cpl Geoff Ardley.*

Remembering the First World War

The Sheringham camp of the King's Own Royal Regiment, Norfolk Imperial Yeomanry, 1907.

A greetings card from a soldier stationed in Sheringham to his wife and son.

A postcard sent in 1915 to a loved one serving far away from home

Members of the Royal Norfolk Regiment. Sergeant H.R. Craske (centre, far right) *later became secretary of the Golf Club.*

Pipers from a Scottish regiment entertain visitors to a charity event in Sheringham Hall grounds.

(A TANSLEY PHOTOGRAPH)

Left: *Pillboxes at the crossroads at Pretty Corner.*

Remembering the First World War

During the First World War The Dales was a convalescent home. This Tansley photograph shows soldiers enjoying a game of bowls.

The funeral of a soldier of a Scots Artillery regiment.

Left: *This Navy seaplane, anchored off Sheringham in 1916, put down a sea anchor and the crew were brought ashore by a local fisherman. During the night there was a storm and the plane was driven ashore.* (A Tansley Photograph)

Weybourne Camp, c.1929. Originally a Territorial Army camp in the 1920s, it grew to a permanent anti-aircraft training centre, with some 250,000–300,000 men passing through and three batteries at a time undergoing training. The last gun was fired on 2 October 1958 and the camp closed in March 1959. Controversy then raged, as the War Department wanted to put the site to industrial use while Norfolk County Council wanted the land returned to agricultural use. Rumours of it becoming a Butlin's holiday camp, a prison, a factory farm, a marina, a nuclear power station or a picnic site ended when restoration work began on the old NAAFI building, and on 7 May 1988 the Muckleburgh Collection was officially opened by the Duke of Argyll. It is now the biggest and, arguably, the best privately owned military museum in the country and one of our major visitor attractions. It also houses a magnificent display on the Norfolk and Suffolk Yeomanry.

Fortunately it, too, failed to ignite. 'London Bill' Barney dashed into the cottage, picked up the bucket and took it outside, where he filled it with water from a nearby tap.

In the 1930s, as the country mobilised for war, gas-masks were issued to every adult and child in the country in readiness for what the authorities believed would be massive gas attacks. So great was this fear that local garages had been earmarked for use as mortuaries, and tens of thousands of sturdy folding cardboard coffins had been stockpiled. The Sheringham Urban District Council was congratulated by a lady for the 'capable manner' in which respirators had been distributed – much more efficiently than in her home town of Thetford.

Despite widespread publicity there was a very poor attendance when the gas van visited Sheringham on the evening of 2 March 1939. Just 24 adults turned up to have their gas-masks tested and be instructed in their correct use.

Similar public apathy appears to have been shown when a combined ARP exercise was held throughout the town on 4 July. Fireworks were used to simulate different kinds of bombs, fires were lit on Beeston Common to represent incendiary bombs, an aeroplane flew overhead and imaginary bombs were dropped close to the War Memorial, as well as in Hasting Lane and Alexandra Road. Rattles were spun and wardens blew their whistles to advise of an imminent air raid and then to advise of the all clear.

There were reported to be 'many' casualties (evident from the number of bodies littering the streets), and it was generally agreed by those taking an active part in the exercise that wearing anti-gas clothing, a gas-mask and a steel helmet was not an ideal way to spend a hot summer's evening.

Whilst no record has been found of the attitude of the onlookers, some insight might be gleaned in the subsequent report to the Council, when councillors asked wardens and special constables to make sure that on any future exercise they 'ensure a more rigid discipline among the civilian population'.

Another Zeppelin Over Sheringham

As we have seen, a Zeppelin over Sheringham could be a frightening experience.

On Friday, 26 June 1936, however, everything was different. As Joan Thirtle has recalled, a teacher came running into her classroom at the town's Infant School, calling out: 'Quickly, children, come outside and see a Zeppelin flying over the town.'

What Joan, the children and many townspeople saw was Airship LZ129, the *Hindenburg*, on its return journey to Frankfurt from Lakehurst, near New York, and miles off course from its usual flight path. The reason for this was both simple and significant. Adolf Hitler originally wanted this airship to carry his name but he was thwarted by the captain, Hugo Eckner, Head of the German Civil Airship Service, who argued that having the dictator's name attached to the airship could alienate passengers on the

Special Constables, Sheringham beat, 1945. Left to right, back row: *D.J Barrows, J.W.L. Barker, J. Cooper, D.E. Robertson, J.W. Craske, W.R. Harrold, H.J.H. Rust;* second row: *P.L. Goward, H.R. Craske, F.H. Bushell, H.R. Lee, C.H. Smith, P.C.G. Turner, B.A. Watts, K. LeGrice, B.V. Yallop, R. Hughes;* front row: *R.F. Hannah, F.T. Joy, C.H.P. Fish, Inspector G.H. Brunson, S.H. Fish, S.E. Clitheroe, W. Collins.*

The Zeppelin Hindenburg *passing over Sheringham High Street on Friday, 26 June 1936.*

transatlantic route. He also initially argued against an order, direct from Hitler, that he should carry a photographer as a passenger. He knew that the purpose of such a passenger was to take photographs of English military and industrial sites. It was only when he was threatened with the transport of himself and his family to Dachau concentration camp that he agreed. He also failed to prevent the painting of the Nazi swastika on the airship's tail fin. To make matters worse, Captain Eckener had to obey instructions from the photographer on where they were to fly. Another, this time welcome, passenger was Max Schmeling, Germany's champion boxer, returning home after inflicting the first defeat on American boxing champion Joe Louis (real name Joseph Louis Barrow), knocking him out in the twelfth round. Louis was avenged in a rematch when he floored the German champion in the first round. On 6 May 1937 the *Hindenburg*, as it approached its moorings, was showing signs of a fire, and within minutes it was engulfed in flames. All 31 passengers and crew lost their lives.

As early as March 1938 the fire brigades of Cromer, Mundesley, Holt, North Walsham and Sheringham agreed to combine to provide a cohesive service both to the urban areas of Cromer and Sheringham and to the scattered villages and hamlets of the Erpingham Rural District Council.

The 5th Royal Norfolk Regiment, Territorial Army, could boast 40 members, 'the pick of the district', and 'all trained ready for anything that might happen'. Local photographer Harry Tansley was Detachment Secretary.

By now Major Tru May was District Organiser/Instructor of the ARP Organising Committee, Section Officer J.A. Draycott was responsible for training newly recruited auxiliary firemen and Bertram Watts, the Scout leaders being on active service, had taken over as Acting Scoutmaster. In 1937 he had been given a First World War prismatic compass and, using this in conjunction with an Ordnance Survey map of the Sheringham area, he could, by taking bearings on local landmarks such as the highly secret radar station at West Beckham, check the accuracy of this treasured possession.

In early 1940 he decided to take his Scouts on an orientation exercise using both map and compass. In those days anyone found in possession of a camera or map was immediately under suspicion as a fifth columnist or spy. So it was with this innocent Scoutmaster when one of the scouts accidentally left the map on a bench, where it was found and handed in to the police. Bertram told me that it was not long before representatives from both the police and the Army arrived at his house, where they gave him a long and intensive interrogation. After they told Bertram, at last, that they were satisfied he was innocent, he inquired what would happen next. He was not reassured by the comment from an Army officer: 'Oh, you'll probably be put against a wall and shot!'.

When the question arose as to how many evac-

Evacuees from St John the Evangelist School in Islington obviously enjoyed their short stay in Sheringham, calling it 'the children's paradise'!

uees the town could safely accommodate, those in authority considered 660 was an attainable number. Having arrived at Great Yarmouth by paddle steamer, the evacuees were then taken to the racecourse, where they were divided into groups and selected to go to their individual foster-homes. Sheringham's allocation was closer to 1,000, mostly from Roman Catholic schools in Islington. Although everyone had pity for the children, the local authorities made it clear they did not consider Sheringham and Cromer safe areas to receive these children, vulnerable as there would be to constant 'tip and run' air raids. To support this view it has to be remembered that as the evacuees were arriving local children were themselves being evacuated.

Local papers were full of reports of the 'culture shock' experienced by Sheringham families hosting children who had only slept on floors, who had few social graces and who were complete strangers to baths and personal hygiene. It is evident, however, that the children enjoyed what proved to be a relatively short stay with their host families. Short because government sources came to accept they had made a mistake in sending vulnerable children to Sheringham, exposed as it was on the east coast. On 2 June 1940 they were put on trains from Cromer to Cresswell in Staffordshire, this being considered a much safer environment. The arrival of so many children had posed huge problems for local schools, who could not cope with the extra numbers. A rota system in which local and evacuated children took it in turns to attend morning and afternoon classes proved cumbersome and difficult to organise, so several of the large empty houses, mostly holiday homes, throughout the town were requisitioned so that classes could be spread across the town – a very wise move when bombs started to fall in the town centre, some quite close to the main school.

The first incident of any consequence to affect Sheringham and remind residents how vulnerable

they were to enemy attacks took place in the early hours of Wednesday, 5 December 1939.

A twin-engined Heinkel 115 mine-laying aircraft, after completing its mission, for some reason came inland, where one of its wings clipped one of the pylons at the West Beckham radar station. It crashed on the West Beach just below the lifeboat house.

The Royal Norfolk Regiment, stationed in the town at the time, were ordered to despatch a guard party to the scene to prevent sightseers and souvenir hunters from disturbing the site. By the time they arrived on the beach some local fishermen had already been and gone; so had the plane's compass and the pilot's seat.

It was discovered that the aircraft's fuel tanks were protected by a hitherto unknown rubberised material, and subsequent examination at the Aircraft Research Establishment at Farnborough proved it is believed, most productive.

The body of the aircraft's Observer, Oberfeldwebel Emil Rodel, was taken to Bircham Newton, where he was buried with full military honours, complete with an RAF Honour Guard, an 11-gun salute and a wreath made up of red carnations, salmon pink and white chrysanthemums, heather and maidenhair, with the words: 'A tribute to a gallant Airman from the officers, NCOs and airmen of the RAF'.

When the body of the pilot, Oberleutnant W. Wodtke was washed ashore several days later, he was

The Heinkel 115 twin-engined twin-float seaplane.

The remains of the Heinkel on the west beach, with the lifeboat house in the background.

In June 1940 the government finally acknowledged that Cromer and Sheringham were not safe places to send London evacuees. Here they are leaving Cromer Station for Cresswell in Staffordshire.

buried in Sheringham's cemetery, again with full military honours – an RAF Honour Guard, the sounding of the Last Post, an 11-gun salute and a single poppy dropped on the coffin by a member of the local British Legion. It has to be remembered that this was still the time of the 'Phoney' or 'Gentleman's' war, when we treated our enemies as we would wish to be treated ourselves. All such chivalrous thoughts were soon to be dispelled.

When Secretary of State for War Anthony Eden issued his historic appeal for men to volunteer to form the body to be known as the Local Defence Volunteers (known irreverently to members of the Regular Army as the 'Look, Duck and Vanish Brigade') over 174 men immediately volunteered to sign on at Sheringham Police Station to form the basis of No. 1 Platoon, No. 1 Company, 13th Battalion Norfolk Home Guard – renamed after Winston Churchill announced his preference for it. One of their first duties was to provide a nightly guard at Organ Beck to watch for any signs of an invasion. A very damp disused brick kiln served initially as their shelter, followed by a platelayer's hut by the railway line to Cromer, then finally their own beach hut on the cliff top. Stores were kept in what was Rudd's upholstery shop in Church Street, later Eddie Page's Goss Cottage Antiques. Later in the war members took over guard duties at the coastal battery on Skelding Hill. They trained on Beeston Common, and Henry Grice has recalled they had to go to Roughton or Holt for petrol as none was available in Sheringham due to invasion fears and the need to deny any invading force a supply of fuel. Initially the Upper Sheringham Home Guard reported to an estate office near the school but then combined with the main town force to jointly patrol the coast road and village, each man being on duty two nights a week.

There is no doubt that some one million men, armed and trained, were a deterrent, and that after Dunkirk these volunteers were, in reality, our first line of defence. They were expected to respond to calls for duty, '... not necessarily fully clothed or equipped', but with enough food to last at least 24 hours.

Whilst the TV series 'Dad's Army' has attained almost cult status, there are always local incidents which can top anything the script writers might come up with. A pompous naval office was inspecting members of the local coastguard. Stopping in front of Donnie 'Ha' Hannah, he asked the simple question: 'What steps would you take, my man, if the Germans invaded?' Back came the laconic, but immediate, response: 'Bloody long uns – Sir.' Everyone there knew he did'nt mean it, but pomposity was duly pricked.

Sheringham, like other towns and villages, had become accustomed to the presence of thousands of troops in their midst. The top floor of B.A. Watts's

At Sheringham cemetery, with verger and cemetery superintendant John Barker (far right) *and undertaker Stephen Clitheroe* (third from right).

The funeral of Oberleutnant Wodke, with members of the RAF acting as pallbearers and honour guard.
(A Tansley Photograph)

The funeral of Oberleutnant Wodke. Note the swastika-draped coffin. Turned to the camera (centre) *is funeral director Stephen Clitheroe.* (A Tansley Photograph)

The 11-gun salute at the burial with full military honours of Oberleutnant Wodke.

Sheringham Home Guard, pre-1942. Left to right, back row: *George Duffield, Billy Bishop, Charlie Knowles, Reg Cooper, Stephen Chastney, Leslie Pestell, Bill Rawlings, Ron Spendloff, W. Colman, Bob Knowles, D. Quinland;* fourth row: *Walter Brown, Charlie Field, ? Parker, John Marling, Donald Tuck, ? Jacobs, A. Rouse, Cyril Bumphrey, P. Bullock, Charlie Basham;* third row: *John Battrick, Bert Seely, George 'Lobster' Farrow, Bert May, George Broughton, Henry Grice, Jimmy Sadler, Billy Steward, Harold 'Corgi' Grice, Jim Stolworthy, ?, Alec Lawrence;* second row: *George Pratt, ? Osborne, Bob Moore, John Ewing, Major Harman, Lt Harold Dyball, Major Spurrell, Major Walker, Freddie Mills, Reg Parker, Dave Downie, Instructor (Regular Army);* front row: *Donnie Long, Ginger Wright, George Wegg, Billy Bayfield, Freddie Thirtle, Sgt Stone (Regular Army Instructor), Bert Lowe, ? Sanderson, W. Champion, Wilfred Bayfield, Billy Lusher, Sgt E. Hicks.*

Admiring glances for the new volunteers! Left to right: Freddie Mills, Harold Dyball, Major Harman Reg Parker, G. Pratt.

The view from Tansley's Studio, Augusta Street, 1940, with the town full of troops and their vehicles.

bookshop and newsagents became a Forces canteen noted for its beetroot sandwiches, whilst Peter's Bookshop in St Peter's Road (one of the best in the region) was a civil defence message-receiving station.

All hotels had been requisitioned and were full of troops and ATS girls, most of the latter working at the anti-aircraft training camp at nearby Weybourne. Bofors guns were sited on the golf club practice ground, the Hazard car park off Cliff Road and the putting green at the top of the same road.

Everyday life had changed in many ways. Pigeon fanciers were told their pigeons could be comman-

deered, postal delivery services were down to two a day (!), the flying of kites was prohibited, attics had to be cleared of all combustible material and restaurants could no longer offer meat and fish dishes on the same menu. You could be fined for not carrying your gas mask, and for smoking in the street. If that was a worry, then the military authorities literally went into a panic when, on 10 January 1940, dozens of foil-wrapped packets containing a mysterious white powder were found scattered across the town by patrols from the 287th Field Company, Royal Engineers. Initially they were thought to be some form of anti-personnel gas powder either dropped from an enemy aircraft or, more worryingly, scattered

Waterbank Road, Sheringham, 1941. Note the wall of the shelter on the left-hand side and the taped windows of the houses. The Parish Hall now stands on the site of the old trench shelter. Left to right: Mrs Annie Farrow, a soldier from the Northamptonshire Regiment, a soldier's wife, a soldier, Mrs Mabel Sharp, John 'Dunny' Hannah, Mrs Adeline Hannah.
(COURTESY MRS A. FARROW)

by fifth columnists living in the vicinity. Troops, properly protected by anti-gas clothing and fitted with rubber gloves, were detailed to collect samples which were sent away to secret destinations for forensic examination. Representatives from Military Intelligence were sent down from London to investigate.

Subsequent enquiries revealed that local Scouts, on their way home from an evening's training, had to pass to the rear of Miss Cicely Sparke's (later Mrs Winn) hairdressing salon at 'Lindy' on the Cromer Road. She had previously told the Scouts they could have the tinfoil provided they did not spill the powder, which she used to set her clients' hair into rollers. The temptation, however, was too great for some of the boys, who realised the packets would make very effective 'bombs' to throw at each other, especially as a direct hit would be readily identifiable. The result of their game was all too clear the following morning; Mrs Winn recalled 'a great commotion' when the spilt powder was discovered. At the time all this made a very good story, and more than one national newspaper thrilled its readers with tales of a sinister white powder dropped on an 'East Coast town'. The same is also true of at least one wartime history book seen by the author.

Members of the Norfolk Regiment install tank traps at the top of Station Road during the Second World War.
(COURTESY THE IMPERIAL WAR MUSEUM)

In early February the town experienced snow drifts some 10–12 feet deep, and it took the combined efforts of members of the 6th Battalion Royal Norfolk Regiment and prisoners of war drafted in from nearby holding camps to keep roadways clear. The extreme weather conditions resulted in several cases of sore throats and influenza, and a temporary hospital was opened in two rooms of the Grand

Skelding Hill on the golf course. The dark patches are entrances into the many tunnels which were used to store shells and a wide range of ammunition.

Members of the Norfolk Regiment at a checkpoint on Cromer Road outside the Morley Club, 21 April 1942.
(COURTESY THE IMPERIAL WAR MUSEUM)

Hotel, with members of the local branch of the Red Cross providing the nursing staff and a 'great deal' of the furniture, drugs and comforts.

Members of the regiment were also busy erecting roadblocks and other defences at all entrances to the town and moving their battle headquarters from 'St Bernards' in North Street.

Skelding Hill, on the golf course, had a honeycomb of tunnels buried within it, these being used for the storage of shells, other armaments and a range of weapons. In the face of the cliff was a 6in. gun taken from the First World War warship *Belfast*. When it was decided, on 20 June, to fire a practice round, the result was so unnerving that the authorities decided that even if there was an invasion this gun would never be fired in anger! Surprisingly, it was not until the late 1950s or early '60s that the tunnels were sealed off, depriving local youngsters of an exciting, but very dangerous, playground.

In July 1940 it became obvious that an invasion was still considered a real possibility, with orders to all military units that there would be no withdrawal from any position. It also became clear that commanders considered the best time to attack an

The 11th Battalion Royal Scots Fusiliers, 1942. **Far left** *is Major A.R.W.C. Montgomery Cunninghame, reputedly the tallest officer and with the longest name in the British Army. He was killed in action in Holland in 1944.* **Second left** *is Lt/Col Walter Syfrett, Commanding Officer RSF.*

Cromer Road, with the remains of Victoria House and the bus stop where Mrs Abbs was killed.

The scene at the rear of houses in Barford Road after the air raid of 22 September 1940. A total of 529 properties were damaged by blast in the raid.

Barford Road, 22 September 1940, with a young Stacey Blyth (rear right) *looking for souvenirs.*

invading foe was to hit them as they disembarked from their landing craft. To this end boffins came up with a very simple idea – in theory at least! It involved filling oil drums with a mixture of explosives, nuts, bolts and nails, putting them on pram chassis, lighting a short fuse and then letting them trundle down the beach toward the invading hordes. It soon became clear, in practice, that prams do not simply roll under their own momentum down a wet beach, and certainly not down the shingle banks which we have above our award-winning golden sands. After several 'near misses' during trials the idea was swiftly abandoned.

The reality of war arrived in Sheringham on 12 July 1940, when bombs were dropped on Weybourne Road. Fortunately there were no casualties, although telephone lines and electricity supplies were severely affected. In early September the situation looked extremely serious. The ominous word 'Cromwell', signalling an anticipated invasion, brought the whole of eastern and south-eastern England to an immediate state of readiness, with the Chief of Staff recommending that all towns between Folkestone and Sheringham be compulsively evacuated. The War Cabinet ignored this advice, the town's population

being told that if there was an invasion it would be too late to move. Unbeknown to us, Hitler had cancelled his proposed invasion plans, but the air attacks on us increased in number and ferocity.

At teatime on Sunday, 22 September, four high-explosive bombs were dropped on Cromer Road and Barford Road. In the former, Victoria House was destroyed and a Mrs Abbs waiting at the nearby bus top for a bus to West Runton was killed. By some quirk of wind direction 529 properties were damaged by the blast, some a considerable distance away in the town centre, where roof tiles were damaged and plate-glass windows shattered.

In all conflicts luck and coincidence seem to play a major role. At 'Thalassa' in St Joseph's Road the Sadler family were about to sit down to an unexpected treat for tea – a tin of salmon received in a parcel from relatives in Canada. Looking out of the window, father, Neddy, actually saw the bombs falling. Without a moment's thought he picked up sons Tony (5) and David (4) and bundled them, and his wife, into the cupboard under the stairs. When the raid was over they came out to find that a piece of shrapnel had come through the window, gone through the dining-room door and continued in a straight line to where Neddy had been sitting eating his tea. Nearby, at 'Sunny Comer' on the comer of St Joseph's Road and Cremer's Drift, Richard and Margaret Le Grice had been naughty and, as a punishment, had been told they could not enjoy their Sunday tea sitting by the fire but must sit at the table. One result of the raid was to shatter the windows in

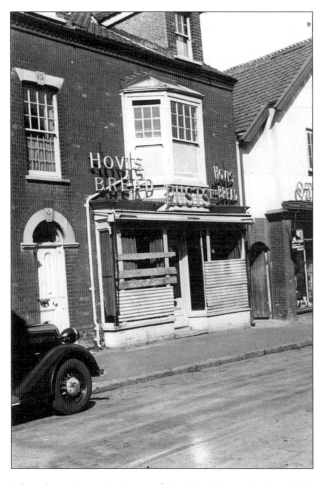

The plate-glass windows of Rust's Bakery in the High Street were shattered by the 22 September blast.

the conservatory, sending slivers of glass into the dining-room, where they imbedded themselves deep into the carpet just where the children would have been sitting eating their tea.

In July 1940 a curfew was imposed on Sheringham, meaning residents could not travel except in vehicles on A and B roads between the hours of one hour after sunset and one hour after sunrise. The Sheringham Hotel became the HQ for members of the 8th Battalion Leicestershire Regiment, who had moved into the town to provide 'greater strength' to the existing defences against an expected seaborne invasion and a land attack from airborne forces. Orders were issued to the effect that:

There will be no withdrawal. The enemy must be met with fire from forward platoons and attacked by reserves so that he will be pushed back into the sea. All ranks will be imbued with the spirit of the offensive form of defence and reserves will be used so as to effect this spirit.

March 1941 was a bad month for Sheringham, with 'tip and run' air raids still frequent. On 6 March a Dornier 17 dropped two high-explosive bombs in New Street and George Street. In the former, postman Stanley Hall and his family were rescued

from a pile of rubble which only minutes previously had been their home. Three other houses nearby were so badly damaged they had to be evacuated. Casualties were a little girl, who was slightly injured, and a man and woman seriously hurt.

Three days later two high-explosive bombs fell in Cliff Road and Avenue North. The former fell in the garden of Major Harman at 'Knowle Side', the second in the garden of 'Two Ways', where Mrs Parker was buried under a collapsed ceiling and general rubble. She was rescued by Dave Downie and was taken to hospital with a broken thigh and hip. The plane then dropped some 200 incendiaries across Beeston Common.

By this stage of the war the Germans were looking for targets other than London, concentrating on the so-called 'Baedeker' raids, resulting in extreme pressure on local fire brigades. Sheringham fire brigade played their part by sending pumps to Cambridge and Romford, and a crew were despatched to help colleagues at Great Yarmouth on 8–9 April 1941.

Two raids on the town on 7 and 10 April saw eight high-explosive bombs falling in an area encompassing The Leas, West Cliff, the beach and Beeston Common. Public services were disrupted and 35 properties damaged.

On 3 May, at 2.40a.m., a Junkers 88 crashed on the West Beach, the crew of four – two of them decorated with the Iron Cross – being taken prisoner by men from the 11th Battalion Royal Scots Fusiliers. One, injured, was taken to Cromer Hospital and on to military hospital at Colchester.

Of all the war years 1942 was to prove the most serious in terms of both frequency of air raids and the number of casualties caused. At a few minutes past six on 19 January a Junkers 88 from Leeuwarden air base in Holland dropped two high-explosive bombs on Cremer Street, demolishing four houses and damaging 262 others, mainly from blast. Four people were killed, three from one family – Mr Smith, his wife and their daughter Peggy. The fourth fatality was a Mrs Rushmer. Eleanor Craske, living in Lawford House in Cremer Street, had engaged Mr 'London Bill' Bamey to redecorate some of her rooms, and in readiness for this he had taken most of the furniture out and stored it in a back bedroom. A large mirror over where she had been sitting at the time of the raid had been blasted off the wall and she was found, after rescuers had tunnelled to reach her, sitting in her chair covered in broken glass and general rubble. When they reached her, her first comment to them was a simple one: 'You'll find the place upside down for I have had London Bill in to do some work.'

On 27 July, at 7.45a.m., a lone Dornier 217 dropped four high-explosive bombs on Priory and Beeston Roads. In terms of civilian deaths this proved to be the most serious of all the raids Sheringham experienced. In Priory Road Nos 27 and

During the Second World War many strange items were washed ashore.

Clearing up New Street after the March 1941 raid.

New Street, 6 March 1941, when a Dornier bomber dropped two high-explosive bombs

'Two Ways', Avenue North, Sheringham. A plaque over the door records that the house was built in 1936, destroyed in 1941 and rebuilt in 1946.

29 received direct hits. At No. 27 Mrs Martins and her two daughters, both in their 20s, were found dead in their Morrison shelter in the garden, it having been blown there by the sheer force of the bomb blast. Nearby, the local fisheries inspector, William Hannah, together with his daughter Elsie and her baby daughter Christine, died. In Beeston Road Mrs Emma Farrow, her daughter Peggy and her baby son David also died in the rubble of their home. Back at No. 23 Priory Road John Craske had gone off to work leaving his wife Elsie and their evacuee boy Joe fast asleep. Uncharacteristically, he had set the alarm and then, instead of leaving it by his and his wife's bed, had placed it under Joe's bed. When Mrs Craske awoke she could not see or find the alarm clock and went downstairs to look for it. As she went back upstairs the siren went, so she woke Joe and together they went into the Morrison shelter. The blast from the bombs lifted up a garden roller, which passed through their bedroom window to land on her and her husband's bed. If she had not

had to go downstairs to look for the alarm clock she could not have told me this remarkable story, or of the impression she got of her house when she reached the other side of the road and looked back.

Although they were not to know it, the last air raid on Sheringham took place on Monday, 19 October 1942, when a Dornier 217, after bombing Cromer, came on to Sheringham and scored a direct hit on a cliff-top property called 'The Retreat', a former school unoccupied at the time of the raid. The plane then machine-gunned surrounding streets without causing any casualties.

Rachel Dhonau and her son Timothy lived in Sheringham all through the war years whilst her husband was away on active service. She was a

In an air raid on Sheringham on 27 July 1942, five people were killed in Priory Road. Very much a 'front line' town, Sheringham suffered 13 major air raids, with 14 people killed and 38 injured and over 600 properties destroyed or damaged.

No. 23 Priory Road after the raid on 27 July 1942.
(A TANSLEY PHOTOGRAPH)

The Retreat, a former school off Vincent Road, received a direct hit but was unoccupied at the time of the raid on 19 October 1942.   (A TANSLEY PHOTOGRAPH)

correspondent for the organisation Mass Observation. They had correspondents across the UK whose responsibility was to keep a daily diary recording their experiences and thoughts of what they were experiencing. Our correspondent was a very articulate lady and not one to mince her words when she thought she had something to say. She worked in the town's Food Office and on one occasion recorded having to write to a food retailer reminding him his current licence was due for renewal. Perhaps even she was somewhat perplexed to receive his reply – that all his 'currents' had fallen off their bushes and he had none left! She was quite critical of servicewomen, especially when she visited her grocer, Bob Durrant, whose shop was where, in 2009, the flower shop is in Station Road, only to find an ATS girl buying the last packet of blancmange that 'would have provided six dinners for her son – and the ATS didn't need them'. To this author her most startling entry is for May 1942 when, after a very disturbed night because of the combined noise of German aircraft attacking a convoy and local military manoeuvres, she records: 'Lots of people got up and went down to the promenade so they should have a good view of the invasion.'

The decision was made, on 27 March 1942, to form a local squadron of the ATC, this being achieved on 31 July the same year. By then 124 boys had enrolled, and it was claimed that the reason for achieving this figure was because no cadet had been rejected at any RAF selection board, although the normal rejection rate was 50 per cent. The Sheringham squadron was unique because, contrary to other squadrons, the local boys, because of their seafaring background, mostly wanted to enrol in the naval cadets and were given a special dispensation to wear a 'Leading Seaman' anchor badge on their left sleeves. Two years after their formation they beat all squadrons from within Eastern Command's seven counties by winning the efficiency trophy, the latter being presented to the Squadron by Air Vice Marshall Leslie Gossage at a ceremony on the Little Links on 4 October 1944.

All through the war years E-boats and U-boats were active, attacking convoys and individual ships as they passed up and down the East Coast. One precautionary measure was the siting, about a mile offshore, of a boom made from rolls of kapok joined together with tennis-ball joints and with strips of metal hanging down into the water ready to foul the propellers of enemy craft. At times of storm and heavy seas parts of the boom could be broken up and washed ashore, providing a continuous supply of tennis balls for local youngsters.

Another highly secret means of defence was the building, on the western slope of Beeston Hill, of a 'Y' Station. Joy Hale from Norwich worked there. She was a fluent German speaker and had volunteered to join the WRNS. Because of her fluency in German

In the Chequers car park, possibly during Wings for Victory week, July 1941. The plane is a Bücker Jungmann BU 131B night ground attack primary trainer and was reputedly brought to England by a Dutch pilot who escaped in it from occupied Holland. Extreme left is J.W. Life (Promenade Inspector), with (far right) Roger Emery.

The flotsam of war. Who were the crew of this dinghy? What nationality were they? Did they land deliberately? Did they survive? Where are they now?

Sheringham ATC. Left to right, back row: Harry Bishop, ?, Stanley Hall, Bob Wink, ?, J. Cubitt, C. Moreton, Dick Fuller, ?, ? Flowerdew, K. Goldsmith, Tony Dennis; third row: Phil Wilcox, Arthur Lewis, H. Creasey, J. Crellin, George Ferguson, K. Farrow, D. Smith, R. Hardingham, J. Tyce, R. Pointer, John Stubbings, Arthur Taylor; second row: D. Craske, R. Russell, W. Little, I. Massingham, S. Blyth, ?, David Sands, ? Nichols, H. Gray, ?; front row: B. Crockford, P. Sadler, G.D. Hayden, H.E. Boyce (OC Holt Flight), S.E. Day (OC Squadron), ? Futter (OC Melton Constable Flight), C.B. White, B. Lowe (Squadron Warrant Officer), Malcolm Griffiths.

she was sent to Coverack in Cornwall for training and, after passing her tests, was posted to Sheringham in January 1943 to join 15 other girls, all fluent in German, whose job it was to listen in to various frequencies and interpret the messages being passed from E-boat and U-boat commanders and between them and their bases. They also listened in to the Elbe-Weser radio stations, who sent out

lifeboats to rescue air crew who had ditched in the North Sea on their return from missions over the UK.

There were two buildings on Beeston Hill; the watch room and adjoining direction-finding tower. Once the girls had determined how many craft were involved and their positions, messages were passed down to either Bletchley Park or Chatham, the latter contacting Harwich, Lowestoft or Great Yarmouth to

An official government propaganda photograph showing one of our defence positions at the Regent cinema facing down Station Road. (COURTESY IMPERIAL WAR MUSEUM)

send out high-speed launches to surprise and attack the enemy boats. Joy told me they stayed at what is now 'Camberly' at the top of Cliff Road, and although they occasionally went to the cinema their requirement to be on duty, collectively, for 24 hours every day left little time for socialising or exploring the surrounding countryside.

Tuesday, 4 January 1944 was to prove a dramatic day for several local people and the crew of Liberator B-24, Serial Number 42-748f 'Alfred' from the USAF base at Wendling. The latter was one of 25 Liberators on a mission to bomb the port and naval docks at Kiel in north-west Germany. In approaching the target 'Alfred' was hit by severe and accurate anti-aircraft fire and by attacking enemy fighters. Power was lost from one engine, the radio was shut down and there was severe structural damage to the wings and other parts of the aircraft.

To add to their difficulties fuel levels were 'desperately low', and it really was touch and go whether they would make it back to base. On the return flight the remaining three engines stopped completely on three occasions, only being restarted by the crew diving and losing height each time. On the second occasion the order to ditch was given, but before it could be implemented the English coast was spotted. Everything possible was jettisoned, and with fuel now virtually all used, the crippled aircraft came in over Sheringham golf links at a height of less than 200 feet, with pilot Lieutenant Colby Waugh desperately looking for a place to land.

By now all fuel had been used with, literally, only seconds left to find an open space. Suddenly a strip of land bordered by pine trees came into view, and it was here that Waugh crashed his plane, with the nose embedded in soft, rising soil. Four of the crew were already dead and another died four days later.

Within minutes local farmer Stanley Wright from Malthouse Farm, West Beckham, Henry West, father

of May Ayers, who had been collecting firewood amongst the trees, and farmworker Charlie Gand were pulling out the dead crew members and helping out the survivors. Meanwhile an ambulance and Dr Lawson had arrived, together with a soldier to mount guard over the wreckage and stop any would-be souvenir hunters invading the site.

Local children Bob Dorey, Jean Garrad and Brian Cooper were also fascinated bystanders.

Doug Willies's superbly researched book *Not Forgotten*, telling the story of this mission, the crew members and their experiences, was published in 1996. So popular did it become that five reprints followed and today only a handful of copies remain. He can be contacted on 01263 825542.

He and his wife Celia, together with May Ayers, were also the moving forces in organising the memorial stone to those killed in this crash, which stands just outside the north door of All Saints Church in Upper Sheringham.

The memorial was dedicated on 7 May 1994 and no fewer than 19 Americans – family members of both the crew who died and those who survived, came to Upper Sheringham to either mourn or give thanks. It certainly demonstrated the special relationship which existed between our two countries, with new friends made and old ones reunited.

When, on 12 January 1943, the Town Council started to consider the postwar planning of the town, the view was already being aired that the Council would 'deprecate' any proposal for the amalgamation of the urban districts of Sheringham and Cromer with other areas which were agricultural in character. Matters really hotted up some two years later when it was suggested that the two councils join to form a completely new authority. The old rivalry between the two towns really began to show – not always through polite correspondence in the local papers!

In Sheringham a meeting was convened on 24 January 1943 at the Infants' School to discuss the future of the town, this leading to the formation of the Sheringham Planning Society, soon to be retitled the New Sheringham Society. On 5 May they presented the results of their deliberations.

Suitable sites for demolition and clearance were 'Ivy Lodge' in Church Street, Cooperative Street to the sea, 'certain houses' in Beeston Road, Cromer Road opposite Brook Hall, Beeston Common and 'White City' opposite the Dunstable Inn. At a further meeting on 7 November they published some quite novel suggestions. First, that by 1999 'most of the houses in Sheringham would be condemned', and that 'improvements' included demolition of the Clock Tower and Little Theatre and all shops as far south as Scotter's fish shop. All this would be replaced by a roundabout linking Augusta Street with New Road, this being realigned to cross Cremer Street to come out opposite the Avenue. Barford Road would be straightened to go south of

Melbourne Road, cut across Station Road and then continue opposite St Peter's Church. All this would result in the demolition of all properties on the south side of Melbourne Road, shops in Station Road from the corner of Melbourne Road to Dawn Fresh greengrocers and from just above Blyth & Wright's to Watson's estate agency, plus those in Waterbank Road, including the Parish Hall, as it continued to the crossroads by the church.

The *North Norfolk News* of 14 April 1950 published a plan of the suggested postwar redevelopment of the town centre. This presumably replaced the radical proposals outlined above, but was itself breathtaking in design and scope. It foresaw the demolition of all buildings from the existing Clock Tower down to the promenade, the resulting empty space being filled with a bandstand, two restaurants, a covered swimming pool, shops and business premises, an ice-skating rink, an exhibition hall, assembly rooms, winter gardens, a dance hall, a youth organisations' social centre, club rooms, a library, an art gallery, a conference hall, a theatre, a Post Office, a telephone exchange, municipal offices, a hotel, boarding houses and apartments, a pavilion, a sports hall, fishing industry buildings, squash courts, a gymnasium and covered tennis courts. The headline above this long list stated that the report took 'a realistic view' of the town centre redevelopment, and elsewhere the comment was made that this redevelopment 'would in no way alter the appearance of the town centre'. Fortunately, in this author's view, the Town Council was unable to raise the necessary funding; otherwise today we would be a mixture of Skegness, Brighton, Great Yarmouth and Blackpool, having completely destroyed the reputation we have as a family resort with an attractive town centre and a range of friendly independent shops.

Immediately after VE Day, on 8 May 1945, a lady achieved national fame by claiming she was the first person in war-torn Britain to enjoy a banana. She, and the national press who reported her claim, were obviously unaware of an event in Sheringham.

Mrs Geraldine Bird (née Smith) remembered the occasion when her father, serving in the RAF, went into Grimsby for a spot of relaxation. Whilst there he met a sailor who sold him a banana. The price was 3s.6d., half her father's pay of 7s. a week.

He brought it back to Sheringham on his next leave and his mother took it in to the Primary School in Cremer Street so that the children could actually see this, to them, rare fruit.

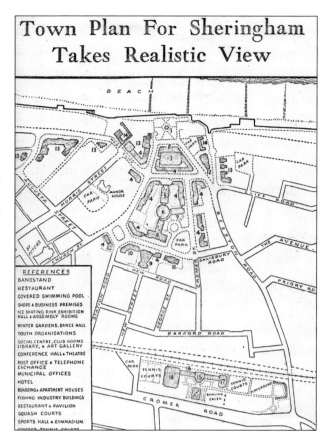

Town Plan For Sheringham Takes Realistic View

She then took it home and mashed it up. The next step was to invite about 20 children to her home, each of them to bring a smallish square of bread and butter on which she would spread some mashed banana.

Among the children were Douglas and Sylvia Bailey, Reg Smith, Teddy Johnson, Pauline and Clive Pigott, Wendy McCann, Ruth Turner, Diane Smith and Rosemary Basham.

Geraldine also recalled the 'lovely community spirit' of the time, with wives taking turns to cook meals in order to save fuel, and never locking doors so you could leave home immediately should an emergency arise.

In the evenings mothers would sit outside on a bench and have a good 'mardle' whilst knitting vests for babies. They would continue until it was nearly dark, thereby giving the items knitted the local name of 'twilight vests'.

Much of the information in this chapter first appeared in the author's book *Coastal Towns at War*, the story of the Second World War in Sheringham and Cromer, now long out of print, published in 1988 by Poppyland Publishing, who have generously given their permission to reproduce it here.

Sheringham Through the Years

Sheringham High Street and Clock Tower, 1910.

Sheringham High Street and Clock Tower, 1916.

Sheringham Through the Years

Sheringham High Street and Clock Tower, 1925.

Sheringham High Street and Clock Tower, 1925.

Sheringham Through the Years

Sheringham High Street and Clock Tower in the 1930s.

Sheringham High Street and Clock Tower, 1950.

Sheringham Through the Years

Sheringham High Street and Clock Tower, 1959.

Sheringham High Street and Clock Tower, 1964.

Sheringham Through the Years

Sheringham High Street in 1862, with just a bank on the right.

Sheringham High Street, 1895.

Sheringham Through the Years

Sheringham High Street seen from the other end, 1908.

... and in 1916.

Sheringham Through the Years

Sheringham High Street, 1934. The International Stores are on the left and 'The Allies' sweet and ice-cream shop on the right, on the corner with Cooperative Street. (COURTESY R.M. HEDGES)

The northern end of High Street in the 1890s, with the Lobster Hotel on the right and Smith's Stores on the left. The only lighting is from the lantern outside the Two Lifeboats Hotel. Note also, there is no sea wall at this date.

Sheringham Through the Years

The northern end of the High Street in the early 1900s. The cottage facing the camera has now become J. Alderton's furnishing store.

The clothes and car date this to the 1950s or 1960s, and Alderton's has become a 'Bargain Centre'.

A beach scene, c.1875, with tents and a bathing machine and everyone dressed to the hilt!

A delightful Edwardian photograph showing people dressed up to go to the beach.

CHAPTER 3

Our Greatest Asset

To the many thousands of visitors we welcome every year a safe and attractive beach is paramount. Firm sands provide an ideal playground for both children and adults, whilst a gentle sloping beach offers safe paddling and swimming, provided we treat the sea with respect and take particular care with inflatables and canoes.

The groynes provide shelter from the prevailing winds and the beach huts accommodation for enjoying the occasional cup of tea and sandwich. Photographs and postcards published over a period of some 120 years are a valuable source of information on changing fashions both on and off the beach. Or, as a visitor to Sheringham Museum once commented: 'In the 1800s you were lucky if you saw an instep. Now you can almost see the step-ins!'

Of one thing you can be sure – there is always something to see on the beach, sometimes full of interest, sometimes tragic; from fishermen preparing their bait and launching their boats to the trauma of seeing a fishing boat capsize within yards of the beach, the cries of drowning men echoing in the ears of wives, sons and daughters as they stand unable to help because of the strong undercurrents of the

waves crashing on the shore. The Henry Ramey Upcher lifeboat shed lists several such instances on the memorial board on display.

Our beaches were, unusually, a source of much valued employment for our fishermen during the long winter months, when weather conditions made it impossible to go to sea. During the 1930s upwards of 500 tons of flints were taken off our beaches every

R. Smith and Harry Childs flint picking.

Just to prove you never know what you might see on the beach – an elephant from a travelling circus takes a dip.

In 1904 upwards of 200 tents could be seen between what is now the Marble Arch slope and the lifeboat house on the West Promenade.

Beach scene, c.1880. Bivouac tents were the first to appear on the beach, followed by the square type, the earliest being a sail wrapped around four oars. Note the second Beeston Bump and the Rocket Brigade's training pole.

The Promenade, c. 1882.

The beach in the late 1950s.

Seen here picking flints are J. H. Pegg (foreman), J. Knowles and J. Bullock.

Weighing and grading the flints.

Sheringham fishermen and their families 'diddling' for coal on Centre Beach following the wreck of SS Hawkwood *on 29 May 1903. Note the women are wearing their traditional shawls.*

In this painting by B.W. Barwell people are gleaning for coal from a ship driven ashore and wrecked on the beach.

winter, the pickers being paid 6s.6d. for every ton picked. It was the blue boulder flints that were required and it was the responsibility of the pickers to provide their own receptacles. This resulted in a motley collection of bags, sacks, trolleys, prams, wheelbarrows and other items being carried, pushed or pulled up the slope to the 'Marble Arch', to an area where the flints were weighed and graded. They were then taken to the railway station and despatched to Stoke-on-Trent, where they were ground to a powder and used to add strength to pottery products, the firm of Shore & Coggins being a major user in their 'English Bell' range of china items. For their part the Urban District Council ploughed back about £850 into the General Rate Fund – equivalent to a 4p rate. No picking was

A team of men dismantling and salvaging what they can from the steamer Commodore, *which remained on the beack for seven years.*

allowed during the Second World War, and it was not until 1960 that it recommenced, this time with about half the tonnage of the pre-war years being removed.

By this time, despite the financial advantages to the fishermen, there were increasing calls for the practice to be discontinued, many local people and environmentalists generally expressing concern that such large-scale removal of stones was affecting the role of the beach as a 'first line of defence' against the ever-greedy sea. After several unsuccessful attempts they finally persuaded the Urban District Council to stop the practice, and in April 1969 the picking of flints off our beaches came to an end. Under the terms of the Coast Protection Act 1949, it is now illegal to remove stone of any description from the beaches and cliffs.

'Picking' of a totally different kind has always been popular with local residents.

The North Sea off our stretch of coast is not known as 'The Devil's Throat' for nothing. Sudden changes in weather conditions can occur at any time, and whilst local fishermen may be able to recognise important tell-tale signs, the captains of much larger vessels will not have the experience or instincts warning of impending danger until they hear the crunch of being driven aground on a foreign beach.

When the SS *Hawkwood* came ashore on 29 May 1903 its cargo of coal was soon scattered across the beach, all ready for local people to go 'diddling' for whatever they could find and carry.

Norwegian rock being unloaded from a barge (top) *to be used as 'rock armour' to dissipate the force of the waves and defend the seawall.*

During the Second World War an even better cargo came ashore – oranges – with no shortage of willing hands to scoop up as many as could safely be carried home.

On the night of 7 November 1896 the steamer *Commodore* was driven by gale force winds to ground on the West Beach just below the Marble Arch that gives access to the promenade.

The *Henry Ramey Upcher* lifeboat was launched the following morning to bring the 14-man crew ashore, and within 24 hours the vessel was a total wreck.

When waves hit a promenade or any other wall it is not just the water that causes damage; it is the debris the water carries – small stones, sand and general rubbish picked up as the waves are moved up the beach. Over a period of time much damage to the fabric of the wall can occur, not all of it visible to the naked eye.

At Sheringham hundreds of tons of Norwegian rock have been placed in front of the promenade to disperse the power of the waves and thereby prolong the life of the protective wall.

Just a word of warning; if you have young children who love to play on the rocks, keep an eye on them and warn them of the dangers of falling down the gaps between.

A Warm Welcome Awaits

A prime prerequisite for an enjoyable holiday is finding a high standard of accommodation and catering at a reasonable cost.

Sheringham prides itself on meeting these requirements, despite losing six of its former hotels - the Dormy House (converted into flats), the Grand (demolished and replaced by blocks of flats), the Sheringham Hotel (converted into luxury apartments), Southlands (closed and awaiting redevelopment), the Station Hotel (converted into offices and flats) and the Loudwater Hotel (replaced by flatted

development). The remaining three hotels, the Beaumaris in South Street, the Burlington on West Cliff and the Two Lifeboats at the northern end of the High Street, lead the way in offering first-class accommodation and catering. They are well supported by a range of guest-houses and private

An imaginative sign from the 1920s!

The Sheringham Hotel.

The Dormy House Hotel.

The Grand Hotel, demolished in 1974.

The main hall, the Sheringham Hotel.

Southlands Hotel, South Street, July 1924.

The Station Hotel, with proprietor Arthur Pretty standing in the doorway.

The Cedars, South Street, incorporated into the Beaumaris Hotel, next door, in 1956

The Beaumaris Hotel, South Street.

The Burlington Hotel.

houses offering bed and breakfast and, in many cases, an evening meal.

It is estimated that Sheringham's population increases three- to four-fold during the summer months, this being due, in no small measure, to the many caravan and camping sites in the immediate neighbourhood.

Fortunately we have a wide range of restaurants and takeaways offering traditional English foods, as well as Indian and Chinese restaurants and take-aways, good pub food and several sources of that

very popular basic dish, good old fish and chips.

Before we look at the fascinating stories of hotels past, some words on our three surviving hotels.

The Burlington Hotel was built in 1899 by the same company that built the former Grand on the West Cliff. The Grand was seen, and was intended to be seen, as one of the finest hotels along the North Norfolk coast.

It obviously did not want competition, so a clause was inserted in the Burlington's deeds preventing the word 'Hotel' being used initially in any of its adver-

Ponies and donkeys for hire outside the Burlington Hotel.

Boys with goat carts and ponies for hire waiting outside the Grand Hotel.

tising or promotional literature. When it opened to the public it was as Burlington Apartments. During both world wars it was requisitioned to accommodate troops, and after 1918 it was known as the Burlington Private Hotel. In later years, following the end of the Second World War, it gradually deteriorated and lay empty and neglected. This continued until the 1900s, when the new owners arrived to start a massive programme of improvement and modernisation. The new hotel opened in May 1997 and includes an extremely well patronised restaurant.

The Beaumaris Hotel has been run by members of the same family for over 60 years and is proud of the high number of guests who return year on year to enjoy the friendly service and high-quality good English cooking.

The Two Lifeboats Hotel has had a chequered career, with a history stretching back over 200 years. It started life as a farmhouse, and Peter Cox, in his book *The Divided Village*, provides a detailed history of its various landlords and their families. In the mid-1800s it was known as the New Inn, with the northern end of the High Street being known as Cliff Street.

The author has seen a reference, not substantiated, that at one time it gained a reputation as a house of ill repute. If true, it could have been during its closure in the late 1870s. It reopened in 1879 as the Two Lifeboats Coffee House, the new name coming from the *Augusta* lifeboat, the town's first recognised official private lifeboat, and the *Duncan*, Sheringham's first RNLI lifeboat, housed in a purpose-built lifeboat house, now known as Oddfellows Hall, on Lifeboat Plain. Blanch Pigott, a granddaughter of Abbot and Charlotte Upcher, continued the family's interest in the premises and was herself succeeded by a Mrs Francis Ives, who continued until the outbreak of war in 1914, at which time the Coffee House closed for the duration.

It reopened as the Bijou Hotel and Café run by Mrs Battle and her daughter, who made such a success of it that elderly residents have recalled their parents passing on memories of lines of cars parked in the High Street as far back as the former reservoir, now known as the Town Clock, at the junction of High Street with Church Street and Station Road.

The first hotel to be built in the town was the appropriately named Sheringham Hotel in 1889 at a cost of £10,000. It epitomised all the grandeur and elegance of the late-Victorian age, with its 120 bedrooms, mostly en suite, 2,000-seat dining-room, two electric lifts and attractive ballroom with its own 'first class orchestra' during the main holiday season. It also offered guests the opportunity to explore 4½ acres of gardens, shady walks and kitchen gardens. The 1935 tariff offered high season inclusive terms varying from 15s. to 27s. a day for stays of not less than three days. 'Inclusive' meant what it said – accommodation, attendance, baths, breakfast,

What is today the Two Lifeboats Hotel was a farmhouse in the early 1800s – the sign in the first-floor window on the right advertises apartments. There is evidence that the gate gave access to steps leading to the beach.

luncheon, dinner, afternoon tea and dances. Visitors' servants were catered for at just 10s.6d. a day, except during August..

Visitors were assured that all members of staff were being paid the maximum wage allowed by the National Catering Board and that the previous 10 per cent gratuity surcharge had been eliminated.

One of the managers, one Stephen Gray, is on record as saying that Sheringham 'enjoys a phenomenal amount of sunshine and is marvellously free from rain'. He even went so far as to offer guests a 'Sunshine Guarantee', which stated that for every sunless day until 21 July and after 10 September a deduction of one-third would be made from their daily inclusive terms. In the event of any dispute as to whether or not a day had been sunless, the parties would abide by the records kept by an official of the Sheringham Urban District Council. In 1984 the hotel was converted into 19 self-contained one- and two-bedroom apartments for the over-50s with a full-time warden on hand to supervise and help as necessary. The original outside appearance of the hotel has been preserved. Although no official records remain, it is known that Princess Alexandra and Winston Churchill were once guests.

The Grand Hotel, built in 1898, dominated the seafront and was acknowledged as one of the finest Victorian hotels along the North Norfolk coast. It was furnished in classic luxurious Victorian style and was the place to stay if you could afford the rates. They may look cheap to us now, but in the early 1900s they did not cater for the average working man. They did, however, provide employment for many local people, including boys, mostly the sons of fishermen, who waited outside with their goat carts to take visiting children for rides round the town.

Like other hotels in the town, it was requisitioned during both world wars and used to accommodate both troops, mainly officers, and ATS girls from the nearby Weybourne anti-aircraft training camp.

The Grand Hotel in 1912, when the managers were Mr and Mrs Louis Holzinger.

The Holzingers changed their name to Hollings after the outbreak of the First World War.

The Lobster Inn, c.1904. The proprietor, M.A Slipper is in the doorway, with Dee Dee Hannah far left.

Prior to the First World War the joint managers were Mr and Mrs Louis Holzinger, a German couple who were interned for the duration, despite the fact that they had changed their names to Hollings.

Toward the end of 1971 it became clear there was an intention to demolish this attractive building, and despite a flurry of objections and a petition signed by over 200 individuals, the die was cast in October of that year when an auction of some 4,000 items from the hotel was announced. Demolition followed in 1974 and the site was redeveloped into square blocks of flats.

The Station Hotel, at the top of St Peter's Road, was in a prime position to catch the attention of visitors who needed a drink and light refreshments after their train journey. It was also a frequent meeting-place for visiting farmers, coalmen and railway staff, who treated it as their 'local'. Arthur Pretty was the landlord for many years and he, together with the bars he controlled, are remembered for their atmos-

A touch of Victorian elegance – the Grand Hotel ball-room.

The Dunstable Arms in the early 1900s, with Mr and Mrs Piper and Annie Shepherd (centre). The stables are on the right.

The Crown Inn, c.1930.

The Sea View Hotel and Restaurant, later Shannocks Hotel, empty and for sale in 2009.

The Robin Hood, a Steward &Patteson house. (COURTESY PHIL SMITH)

The Pretty Corner tea garden, 1922.

phere, heavy with cigarette smoke with all surfaces tinted brown through exposure to nicotine.

The Lobster Inn was originally a coaching inn with its own stables. Elmer Breeze was landlord in 1836. George Emery subsequently held the licence for ten years before becoming a fisherman. The man in charge in 1875 must have been a glutton for punishment, for not only did he run the inn, he was also a hay dealer and a watchmaker. Mathew Arthur Slipper was the landlord in 1888, and in 1897 the brewery company Steward & Paterson bought the freehold. The Crown Inn is the third to stand on the site, the first disappearing over the cliff on the night of 22 October 1800 during a storm. The replacement was built some five years later only to face an uncertain future, with land between it and the cliff edge being eroded at an alarming rate. A severe storm on the night of 30 January 1877 washed away a stretch of the seawall, a cottage and a shed tumbled down to the beach and the inn was deemed to be in an unsafe condition. Repairs were carried out but the threat continued, despite improvements and additions to the seawall and coastal defences. In 1935 the brewery owners decided the long-term solution was to build a new inn further back from the cliff, and this is the inn we see today.

The Robin Hood in Station Road has had a variety of names. Built in 1842, it started life as a beer house with Matthew Jordan holding the licence. He was also a fish curer and partner in a carrier business providing a weekly delivery service to and from Norwich. The 1871 Census names the inn as The First and Last, whilst ten years later it was known, slightly prematurely, perhaps, as the Railway Tavern. Within a few years it had attained the title of the Railway Hotel. In 1904 the then landlord, William Winn, for whatever reason, changed the name again to the present one. On 9 July 1991 the *North Norfolk News* carried the following news item:

Every Friday at 11a.m. Mrs Edna Ashley, Landlady of the Robin Hood pub, marches across the street with a bread pudding for the cast of the show at the Little Theatre. This tradition started about seven years previously when a hungry and penniless actress from the cast went to ask her for crusts from the pub's sandwiches. Mrs Ashley made a bread pudding from them and took it to her.

The Dunstable Arms pub on the Cromer Road opened in the mid-1880s, the landlord being James Woodrow Dennis. Like others in the licensed trade, he also had a second job farming some 16 acres. He was there for about 15 years, his successor being Robert Gray who, after a relatively short period, was succeeded by another two-job licensee, Robert Denis. During his 20-year occupancy Dennis also worked as a general labourer.

✦ CHAPTER 4 ✦

The Sporting Life

The Golf Club

As we have seen elsewhere, the arrival of the railway in 1887 was the catalyst that changed Sheringham from a somewhat backward village into a thriving and developing town. The rich and powerful came to built large second homes, while others came to holiday and explore this new resort. But they all needed 'something to do', and in many cases this meant a round of golf.

The existing course was founded in 1891 on land immediately west of town belonging to the Upcher family of Sheringham Hall, and Arthur Hamilton Upcher became the club's first captain in 1892. The course originally had nine holes and was extended to 18 holes in 1898.

The management were obviously keen to attract visitors to the course, and could well have been pioneers in negotiating package deals with such outside bodies as the Midland & Great Northern and the Great Western railways.

These deals enabled travellers from any station between Sheringham and King's Lynn to travel here for just a shilling, the ticket valid for two days; just

enough time to get in a round or two! The same offer was available to passengers travelling via Great Eastern trains from Lowestoft, Great Yarmouth, Norwich, Wells, Lynn, Foulsham and intervening stations to Sheringham. Travellers from King's Cross, Liverpool Street and St Pancras could enjoy an eight-day golfing break in Sheringham for just 13s.6d., third class. It was emphasised that such tickets would only be issued to those travelling

Sheringham golf links, seventh green, with a rare view of the Old Hythe lifeboat house (left).

Sheringham Golf Club Artisans' Championship in the mid-1950s. Left to right, back row: E. Risebro, H. Grice, R. Baker, F. Farrow, C.C. Forsdick, B. Hannah, S. Childs, W. Emery, R. Green, C. Cooper, B. Newstead; front row: H. Craske, R. Newstead, The Hon. Lady Westerna, A. Makail, Alec Farrow (with a one handicap, winner of the cup), Jimmy Cooper, A. Green, Sir Danver Osborne, E. Kennedy.

Henry John Prince, caddy master at the Golf Club.

Sheringham clubhouse, 1917.

Sheringham Golf Club and caddy house, 1917.

'exclusively for the purpose of playing golf'. Presumably a set of clubs in the luggage was sufficient evidence of intent!

Unlike many other clubs, Sheringham welcomed lady members from the start, Mrs Horace Stopford being the first lady captain in 1894. Significantly, too, a children's course was added in 1899, with youngsters between the ages of eight and 14 and the sons and daughters of members paying just l0s.6d. a year.

Today the Sheringham Golf Club is known as one of the best in the country, renowned for protecting the anonymity of the growing number of national, international and titled golfers who play here.

The Football Club

Notes kept by Stanley Craske show that Sheringham Football Club was founded in 1889 when employees of Bardwell Bros, a building firm from King's Lynn, came to Sheringham to build properties in Cromer Road. Three of the men who came to work here were playing members of Lynn Football Club and encouraged some of the local lads to form their own team to play others from nearby villages. Stanley has given some of the names of the first ever football team to represent the town – G. Evans, Seaman Storey, Billy Storey, Albert Storey, Jimmy Sadler, Bob Bird, T. Sharpins, G. Bennett and Fred Craske.

During the 1900/01 season a Sheringham junior team won their class cup, defeating 'the much famed Lynn North End team' 5–1. This time the team included Herbert Palmer, Billy Grice, Tom Mathews, Jack 'Tar' Bishop, C. Strickland, W. Long, Fred Craske and Joe 'Arch' Pegg. It was around this time that unconfirmed reports name a young Henry Upcher (later Sir Henry) as playing at centre half for the home team and being, by all accounts, 'a rare, rough, handful'.

The opening of the football stand, Holt Road Recreation Ground, 1921. From left to right: Revd G.I. J. Cushing (Methodist Minister, Beeston Road), Miss W. Rollings (later Mrs Stanley Craske), Vincent Smart, W.T. Rollings, H. Mindham (in background), Henry R. Johnson (Club President), ? Woodrow, P. Hammond-Smith, ?, H.H. Palmer, ?, Charles Bouttell, ?, Dave Downey.

Sheringham Football Club, 1902, with Jack Palmer (extreme left, front row), *and in the back row J.H. Bishop* (third from left), *H.H. Palmer* (fifth from left) *and J. Pegg* (seventh from left).

The Butchers' and Bakers' football teams. Traditionally they played every Good Friday. Left to right, back row: Walter White, Alfred Lee, Fred Lusher, George Dennis, ? Minot; third row: James Phillips, William Lusher, 'Busto' Rodgers, William Lambert junr, Bob Olley, Jack Black, William Catchpole, George Youngs, George Emery, Frank Felmingham, ? Saul, Tom Austin; second row: William Tuck, ? Swizle, William Lusher senr, George Algar, Cdr Douglas King RNVR, Charles Dickens, Alfred Wright, Fred Whitear; front row: James Bain, Victor Craske, Charles Thirtle, Hue Wright, ? Painter. Cdr King, who lived at the Dales, Upper Sheringham, drowned in a yachting accident off the Cornish coast and, according to his wishes, his ashes were scattered on the sea, this being carried out during a service aboard the J.C. Madge.

Beeston United, winners in the 1911/12/13 seasons. Left to right, back row: *J. Craske, ?, C.W. Dennis, R.J. Cox, ?, ?, H. Craske, ?, F. Felmingham;* middle row: *Barney Dennis, Jimmy Kemp, Arthur Duffield, ?, C. Holsey;* front row: *Arthur Farrow, ?, J. Bane.*

Sheringham Wednesday football team, 1925. Left to right, back row: ?, ?, John Smith, Geoffrey Gardner, Charles Lambert, Sid Hastings; middle row: Eric Brown, Jack Smith, John 'Ninny' Craske, George Bishop, Henry Dale; front row: Henry Bishop, Bobby Sharpe. The team traditionally played a team from Cromer on Boxing Day, and if things were going badly against Cromer it was not unknown for one of their players to 'stage-manage' a fall in the Sheringham penalty area – not always successfully!

The town's main rivals were, however, the Cromer Crabs team, and the author has heard dire tales of fights both on and off the pitch, and of the windows of visiting coaches being broken by stone-throwing supporters of the home team. As Stanley has recorded:

Many tales have been told of battles royal between the two teams and their supporters when, by the final whistle, the pitch bore a remarkable resemblance to a battlefield.

It is only right, at this point, to say that if a tragedy occurred involving a lifeboatman or fisherman from either town, then the two communities came together in mutual support and prayer.

Early football pitches were at the Weybourne end of the Sheringham golf course, close to Links Road and at the top of Cremers Drift.

Some Sheringham footballers went on to play at a higher level. Joe Hannah was born in Sheringham on 30 November 1898 and from an early age was always happy when playing ballgames. He went on to join the town team, gaining recognition for his consistency and dedication.

In 1920 he was recruited by the Canaries and during his 14 years with the club moved from being a 'stand-in' striker to full back, a position he held for 10 years. Joe was not a happy man if he considered his playing had been below his own strict standards

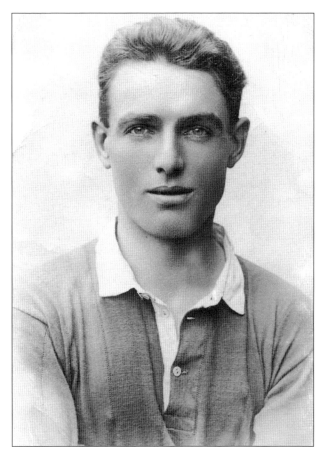

Joe Hannah.

Left to right, back row: *Joe Hannah, Richard Knights, Roy Craske, Stanley Dennis, Brian Algar, John Simpson, Richard Hack*; front row: *Mike Crow, Andrew Turvey, ? Newlands, Geoff Shepherd, Bob Farrow, Alan Beasy.*

(COURTESY PETER BACON)

Beeston United Football Club, winners of the Norfolk Junior Cup in the 1926/27 season. (A TANSLEY PHOTOGRAPH)

Sheringham football team, 1926/27. Left to right, back row: *J. Hall, Jess Howlett, D. Long, ?, Lou Denis, ? Harrison, Herbert Palmer, Jack 'Tar' Bishop;* middle row: *'Shrimp' Brook, Arthur 'Kruger' Farrow, L. Rice, Tom Gray, Charlie 'Kaline' Woodhouse;* front row: *Jack Battrick, ?* (A TANSLEY PHOTOGRAPH, COURTESY PETER BACON)

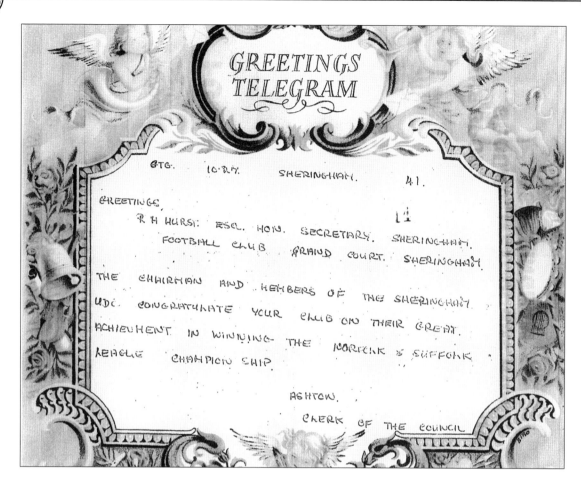

Sterry Cupwinners, Norfolk and Suffolk League, 1957–58. Left to right, back row: *Bill Morris, R. Hurst, R. Goldsmith, B. Pegg, L. Bayfield, V. Farrow, G. Grand, D. Goldsmith, Cyril Plummer, Mr Godfrey;* front row: *John Nichols, 'Nibs' Rawlings, M. Childs, J. Leverington, K. Pegg, A. Beasy, G. Heir, A. Piggott.*

(A Tansley Photograph, Courtesy Peter Bacon)

The last match played at Holt Road Recreation Ground, May 1987, 1st Team v. Ex-players: 1st Team. Left to right, back row: *Bob Horne, Martin O'Leary, Kevin Lambert, Steve Gladman, Dean Stratton, Steve Stacey, Andy Ridley, Mal Gleave, Chris Day;* front row: *Mason Newlands, Mike Blackman, Richard Dromey, Phil Ince, Robin Gleave, Carl Sayer, Bernard Smith.* (COURTESY RICHARD CHILDS)

The Ex-players in the same match as above. Left to right, back row: *Bob Ayers, Mike Childs, Reg Love senr, Roger Pointen, Mike Hurst;* third row: *Ron Shepherd, Arthur Sayer, Derek Sayer, Jeff Piggott, Harry Lewis, Stanley Childs, Mick Howell, ?, Howard Pratt, Pat Underwood, Eric Edwards, Graham Howard, Len Waldron, Fred Duffield, Reg Love junr, Keith Pegg, Mick Gee, Reg Hurst, Brian Pegg;* second row: *Jim McKail, Bruce Cunningham, Paul Scott, Alan Beasy, Peter Bullen, Barry McMahon;* front row: *Stuart McLean, Dick Childs, Colin Grand, Tony Owen, Keith Rudd, Ron Crowe.*
(COURTESY RICHARD CHILDS)

These members of Sheringham Football Club entered for a half marathon from Aylsham to Norwich Cathedral on 3 May 1989. Left to right, back row: S. Stacey, M. Gleve, Charles Hall, S. Walton, Bob Ayers, D. Dancaster, M. Fisher M. Bacon, K. Lambert; front row: R. Dromey, J. Carly, M. Newlands, C. Sayer, B. Smith.

(COURTESY PETER BACON)

Reserve Team members, 1990/91. Left to right, back row: A. Beasy, S. Smith, D. Ellis, G. Attew, Mark Bullen, M. Bacon, M. Gleave; front row: A. Galley, M. Boggis, P. Ince, M. Jimson, T. Goodfellow, P. Wegg.

(COURTESY PETER BACON)

of performance. On one occasion he decided to punish himself for playing below par; he walked the 25 miles home to Sheringham from Norwich. Perhaps it worked because Joe went on to be awarded two benefit matches and was chosen to play for England against Australia.

Sheringham team members Charlie Woodhouse and Joe Pegg also went on to play for Norwich City.

The Cricket Club

Sheringham Cricket Club, like its footballing cousin, can trace its history back over 100 years, with teams originally playing on a ground at Upper Sheringham owned by the Upchers. Until 1946 all matches played by the club were friendlies against local clubs such as Cromer and Overstrand. After this time the first XI played 'good quality friendlies', whilst the 2nd XI played in the local league. Both the football and the cricket club played regularly on the recreation ground on the Holt Road. This was a 10-acre site managed by the Recreation Ground Association, a body newly formed to promote sport in the town. With this in mind it was designed to provide football, hockey and cricket pitches, bowling greens, a croquet lawn and 16 tennis courts. It was also where the annual carnival procession finished its tour of the town with stalls, entertainment and a happy carnival atmosphere, long remembered after the event.

Sadly, the ground was sold by the North Norfolk District Council in 1987 to raise funds to develop the Splash Leisure Centre on the Weybourne Road. Although the District Council promised to provide a replacement recreation ground it was to be some eight years before it materialised. It was on the Weybourne Road, and initial problems with poor drainage and the migration of stones and fragments of glass to the surface of the proposed pitch sites meant a lengthy delay before the ground could be safely used.

In the meantime the town's football and cricket teams lived a nomadic life, travelling from pitch to pitch outside the town. Among the sites used was that of the present High School, Bodham playing-field, Sheringham Hall, Piccadilly Park (Sunway Park) and the Common. Credit must go to the cricket club for their initiative in arranging away matches at venues in Essex, Nottinghamshire, Yorkshire, Cheshire and other counties. With family members accompanying the players, these outings provided vital experiences to all involved and resulted in a bonding that would not have happened if they had

Sheringham Cricket Club, c.1930.
(PHOTOGRAPH BY ALBERT W. COEN)

simply played matches locally. They also kept the club alive and active during the nomadic years. When the new recreation ground opened in 1995 the club quickly became champions of Division 1 of the Norfolk League, gaining promotion into the Alliance and winning the Lady Mary Trophy to qualify for the Carter Cup. It has a vibrant youth section with teams for nine, 11, 13–15 and 17-year-olds. In 2008 the under-13s came seventh out of 1,700 teams taking part in a knock-out competition. The same year Norfolk was represented by nine Sheringham club members in different age groups and in 2009 the first XI was in Division of the Alliance League after two successful promotions in consecutive seasons. The club attained the title of a Clubmark and Focus Club and is recognised by the English Cricket Board as a front-runner in the development of youth cricket.

It was around the time of the nomadic years that Beeston United and Sheringham Wednesday appeared on the scene, the latter getting its name from the fact that for most of its members Wednesday afternoon was the only time they could get away from work. It has also been claimed that this period saw 'an explosion' of interest in football, with upwards of 30 teams, mostly young, playing in and around Sheringham. Today the tradition of youth football is still strong, with the Sheringham Warriors under-14 team, the Sheringham Youth under-14 team and the Sheringham Youth under-15 team providing fully trained youngsters eager to join the town's senior team, who in 2009 again won the Sterry Cup.

Both the football and the cricket club are always eager to welcome volunteers, either as players or as backroom staff, without whom clubs such as these would find it hard to survive.

CHAPTER 5

Keeping the Faiths

Sheringham is fortunate in having nine separate faiths available for its residents' religious needs. Indeed, religion is a strong thread to be found weaving its way through generations of Sheringham residents, whether they lived in the small original village of Upper Sheringham or in its expanding offspring, Lower Sheringham.

The Domesday Book of 1086 records the presence of a church in Upper Town, all traces of which have since disappeared. The present church of All Saints dates from the mid- to late-fourteenth century, as evidenced in the chancel, the font, with its traceried bowl and eight columns, the piscina near the altar and the tower. An excellent small guide provides a wealth of information on what to look for. The size of the church is evidence that it once served a much larger congregation than today, this being confirmed by a walk through the graveyard, where can be seen the names of many fishermen whose descendants still live in the town of Sheringham. Look out for the two green men on the bosses on the underside of the rood screen floor. This is where the deacon stood to translate the Roman Catholic prayers and other passages from the Order of Service for the benefit of the congregation in the body of the church. Look, too, for the legendary little mermaid associated with this great church. The story is told that whilst swimming in the sea off 'Syringham' (which dates it to around AD1230) she developed a great desire to visit this particular Parish Church. After struggling the 1½ miles from the beach she timidly knocked on the church door and opened it. She was met by a very irate beadle, who told her: 'Git yew arn out. We can't hev noo marmeads in hare,' and slammed the door in her face. This little mermaid, however, was a very determined one, and when no one was about she came back to find a permanent home. She is still there today – find her on the end of a pew near the church door. Look, too, for the many memorials to the Upcher family of Sheringham Hall, benefactors to the people of both Upper and Lower Sheringham.

All Saints was enlarged in around 1450 so that it could conform to the Perpendicular style prevalent at that time. It continued to be the Parish Church for both villages until Lower Sheringham attained its title of Parish Church.

As we shall see in Chapter 9, Arthur Wilson Upcher had been responsible for the building of a Chapel of Ease in Lower Sheringham, this being opened on Saturday, 23 January 1842. Whilst it has been referred to as the town's Parish Church, this was only true until St Peter's was built and consecrated.

It was designed by St Aubyn & Wadling of London, built at a cost of £8,000 by Bardell Bros of King's Lynn and stands on about three-quarters of an acre of land donated by the Upcher family. It is one of the relatively few churches to provide chairs for its congregation, the oak for the originals coming from the Sheringham estate and the chairs themselves being made by inhabitants of the workhouse at Upper Sheringham.

The foundation stone was laid on St Peter's Day 1895 by Mrs Upcher, and after two years of building work Sheringham's new church was consecrated on St Peter's Day, 29 June 1897, thereby becoming the daughter church of All Saints at Upper Sheringham. It was not until 1953, when there were ecclesiastical boundary changes that associated All Saints Church at Upper Sheringham with Weybourne, that St Peter's Church in Lower Sheringham became the town's official Parish Church.

With good acoustics, it is a favourite venue for concerts, and the author still has memories of when celebrations were planned to raise money to fund the town's Christmas lights. Torrential rain meant they had to be cancelled, but the day was saved when the organisers were invited to stage their event in the church. As a result, marionettes twirled in the aisles, appropriate jokes were told from the pulpit, stalls enjoyed good takings, musicians played their hearts out, street entertainers entertained and a very good time was enjoyed by everyone lucky enough to be there. To this author it was what a church should be; not just a place for worship but a place for people to enjoy and bring them closer to God.

The Catholic Church in England has grown from a religion whose priests and believers met in secret to avoid recognition and who suffered crippling additional taxation, possible arrest, imprisonment and, in

Sheringham boulevard and St Peter's Church.

severe cases, torture and execution. This was equally true of Catholics living in such primitive seaside villages as 'Schyringhamas', as Sheringham would have been known in the sixteenth century.

At the time of the Reformation Sheringham would have been a small, untidy collection of rudimentary dwellings, records of which list the names of people and identify them as Papist believers; this would have been mainly on the grounds that they refused to take communion at the then local church.

If they dared to worship they most likely met in the homes of such famous families as the Pastons at Barningham and Pudding Norton, the Bedingfields at Oxburgh, the Jerninghams at Costessey and the Duke of Norfolk at Norwich.

It was not until the Catholic Emancipation Act of 1829, which relaxed some of the more insupportable

Catherine Louise Deterding.

(Copyright Jane Valsler)

The building of St Joseph's Catholic Church.

(Copyright Jane Valsler)

restrictions on Catholics, that they could once more worship openly and join the wider religious world.

Clement Scott of Poppyland fame was a prime mover in securing a revived Catholic presence in North Norfolk. He had appealed to the Bishop of Northampton for a priest to attend at Cromer during the summer months to preach both to local worshippers and to the growing number of visitors who brought their faith with them. This, in turn, led to demands for the provision of a Catholic church in the area.

A site was found just outside Cromer, but because of strident local opposition plans were put on hold until an out-of-town site was found on the Overstrand road.

In Sheringham, as at Cromer, local opposition prevented any town centre site being found, so it was, again, a question of finding one on the edge of town. It was not until 1906 that the present site was found on the Cromer Road, the intervening years seeing Mass held in a private home rented by Catholic visitors to the town.

The original chapel, built in 1909–10, is now the side chapel used for weekday Mass and as an overflow during the summer months.

As local worshippers were too poor to pay for the building of a new church it was left to the generosity of Mrs Catherine Deterding, wife of the managing director of the Royal Dutch Shell Oil Co., to give money both to buy the present site and to build the church which stands there today.

It was designed by the architect Sir Giles Gilbert Scott and is the only listed building in Sheringham.

In 1912 30 local children of school age were attending Mass; two years later St Joseph's Elementary School was built next to the presbytery, with Miss Hart the only teacher. In 1921 Sister Teresa McCabe was appointed head teacher and remained in post until the school closed in December 1934. Religious knowledge was the main subject taught. What had been the school was converted into parish rooms which provided a centre for whist drives, bazaars, fêtes and billiards. The school reopened in 1947 with Miss Rose Snowden as head teacher. It closed for good in 1963, the children then going to Sheringham Primary School.

At the same time Scott was commissioned to design a house known as The Close and fronting on to Cremers Drift. This was used originally as the presbytery. When seven nuns arrived in Sheringham in 1921, No. 1 Cremers Drift became known as St Mary's Convent, opened in 1922 for boarders and day pupils. In 1930 the house was extended and connected to the original house, the whole containing a chapel, a schoolroom, a small concert hall, a music room, classrooms and bedrooms. The convent and school closed in June 1940, reopening in 1944 as a home for unmarried mother and babies. The capacity of 28 babies was soon reached, with a waiting list of 20 more.

One solution was to extend the nursery into the property next door, previously known as St Hilda and the home of Benjamin Cooper and his family.

Methodism began as an evangelical movement within the Church of England, but the indifference and hostility of the Church hierarchy led to the formation of a separate denomination. This, in turn, led to the formation of two main groups; the Primitive Methodists liked lively, emotional services and supported radical political ideas and the legalisation of trade unions, whereas the Wesleyan Methodists preferred formal worship and had conservative political ideas.

There were Methodist preaching places in both Upper and Lower Sheringham as early as the 1820s, with travelling preacher William Braithwaite a frequent visitor. There was a Wesleyan chapel in Upper Town by 1836, the biggest local support coming from the fishing community.

In Lower Sheringham in 1844 the Primitive Methodists and the Wesleyan Society built a large chapel in Pratt's Yard, at time of writing the site of the Royal Mail Depot in New Road.

A leading figure in this arm of the Methodist faith was Robert Long, coxswain of the *Augusta* lifeboat, fisherman, preacher and part-time teacher at the school on West Cliff, Lower Sheringham, built and

Beeston Road Methodist Chapel, after its convertion to residential use.

Members of Beeston Road Methodist Church. Left to right, back row: *David Starling, Brenda Edwards, Shirley Reynolds, Joan Temple, Shirley Knowles, Joyce Rix;* middle row: *Robin Facey, Christopher Cooper, Roger Chambers, Roy Craske, Brian Jarvis, Michael Wesh;* front, kneeling: *Tony Colman (Labour MP for Putney).*

funded by Mrs Charlotte Upcher. An existing chapel in Station Road, on the corner with New Road, was closed in 1882, although it was subsequently used for Sunday-school classes with fishermen as teachers.

In Lower Sheringham the Free Methodists worshipped on the site of what is now Salisbury House (built 1891) and situated on the corner of Salisbury Road with Beeston Road. Further down Beeston Road they built their first chapel in 1859 on land acquired from Squire Cremer of Beeston Hall. Flints from the beach were used in its construction, these being knapped by men from the Storey and Sadler families. Some burials were made under the church floor with others, until 1892, in the small graveyard which surrounded the building. Early

Primitive Methodist Chapel, Station Road, built in 1882, demolished in 1966.

Members of Station Road Primitive Methodist Chapel on the occasion of an open-air synod on Beeston Common.

At a Primitive Methodist fête in the early 1930s. From left to right: Walter Starling senr, Walter Starling junr, Colin Turvey, Jimmy 'Mullet' Middleton, Willy Long, C. Middleton, Alfred Neal. The cat, name unknown, is enjoying a bit of fresh crab!

Beeston Road Primitive Methodist Chapel, c.1952. Left to right, back row: *Stanley Craske, John Smith, Arthur Nicholls, Roy Craske, Mabel Pearcy, Winifred Craske, Joyce Smith;* middle row: *Clarice Lee, Ethel Brownsell, Olive Rix, Sheila Temple, Ethel Hopewell, Edith Clarilf, Joan Temple;* front row children: *Alfie Dixon, Brian Vigger, Hilda Dixon, Valerie Frazer – all from the National Children's Home. The choirmaster is Malcolm Rix.*

preachers included such familiar names as Bob 'Tar' Bishop, B. Barsham, John Gladden Craske, H. Storey, R.E. Gray, J. Leake and Robert 'Gofather' Pegg. The chapel closed in 1968 and was converted into a private development.

The Methodist Union in 1932 sowed the seeds for Methodists seriously to consider surrendering their long-held individual forms of worship, combine for the common good and build a new church so that all branches of their faith could worship together. It was a suggestion made more attractive to local Methodists by the knowledge that: maintenance of their chapels was becoming ever more expensive, with the roof of the Station Road chapel rapidly approaching a dangerous condition. It was also felt that by combining the different streams of Methodism this would make the faith more attractive to the general public and attract new members. St Andrew's Church on the Cromer Road was opened and dedicated on Saturday, 22 June 1968, just nine months after the laying of the foundation stone. The Station Road premises was sold off and demolished to make way for shops and flats. The Beeston Road chapel was also sold for conversion to residential use.

A fine example of Christian unity and inter-faith co-operation was the offer by the Revd L.G. Sturman to make St Peter's Parish Church and its hall available for worship and use by Methodists during the uncertain period when chapels were being sold and the new church was being built.

Trustees of the new church included Roy Brownsell, Stanley Craske, Norah Perry, Leslie Willmott, Peter and Betty Rackham, Sidney Hill, Colin Turvey, Walter and David Starling, Billy and Gertrude Felmingham, Laura Hall, John Myer and Dick Rix.

The first moves toward establishing a Baptist Church in Sheringham were taken at a meeting on 3 November 1929 at the home of Miss Buckingham in Cremer Street. She made her home, Cossey House, available both for further meetings and for services, the first of the former being on Friday, 8 November 1929, and the latter on 17 November, when Stanley Hall preached to a congregation of 16 people; the collection raised £1.8s.7d. Further meetings, both religious and secular, resulted in the decision being made, on 6 January 1930, that a Baptist Church should be built in Sheringham, but it was not until 1932–33 that positive efforts were made to find a suitable site.

The official opening of the Baptist Church on 9 April 1952. Left to right: Mr F. Jordan (Chairman of Sheringham UDC), Mrs Jordan, Miss Lacey, Revd Slaughter, Miss Bradford, Revd Clifford Askew, Mr Dorak, Anita Dorak, Revd Gilbert Lawes, Mrs Dorak, Mrs Wheeler, Revd J. Perry Davies, Mrs Clayton, Miss Chastney, Mrs Mildred, Revd Wheeler, Mr Mildred, Mr Clayton.

CSM J. Pegg at the dedication of the Baptist Church.

(COURTESY BRIAN PEGG)

The Baptist Church, from a drawing by Tom Armes.

Although new members to the cause were being recruited, a meeting held on 16 September 1937 was told of 'the sad condition of the church and the evident indifference'. Three months later the pastor, Revd R.C. Law, resigned: 'In order to bring the case of our church before the Baptist Union and highlight the unsatisfactory situation and lack of progress being made.' On 27 May 1939 the deacons recommended that steps be taken to purchase the present site in Holway Road, despite the fact the purchase price was £285 and there was only £65 in the building fund. Two months later a deposit of £28.10s.0d. was paid to the estate agent, Mr R.A. Knight. The

Wives and children from USAF base at Sculthorpe being entertained by members of Sheringham Baptist Church.

purchase of the site was finally completed on 13 October 1939.

On 10 April 1951 the Building Committee reported difficulties with planning permission, the tenders received were deemed too high and there was concern with the rising costs of materials and labour. The decision was made to reduce the size of the new church.

Local company Bullens of Cromer started work on the site on 1 October 1951 at the agreed price of £3,785. The stone-laying ceremony followed on 14 November and the new church was officially opened on 9 April 1952.

On 6 November 1960 a wooden hut, bought from Weybourne Appliances at a cost of £500 and known as the Unwin Hall, was dedicated by the pastor.

By 1975 the hall was showing signs of ageing, and work on extending the main church building was proceeding well. Thanks to the building contractor, Sheringham Development Co., and to Mr. F. Pegg, were placed on record for making such good progress with the construction work.

The YESU New Wine Church was established in Sheringham in 2002, making its presence felt in what had previously been Lusher's Bakery and shop on the corner of High Street and Wyndham Street. Talking to their leaders it is clear they see themselves as a 'people' organisation, with an almost evangelical desire to get out into the community to spread the Christian message and help in any way they can to make this small corner of Norfolk a better place in which to live and work.

Their many faceted programme of events includes parenting courses and support, drug and alcohol advice and support, career advice, debt help and clubs for the 8–11 and 11–14 age groups. Special attention is paid to improving the quality of life for young people, helping them to feel valued and deal with such problems as bullying and absenteeism. At the time of writing they hold sessions and courses at Cromer Junior School.

The Canaan Christian Centre arrived in Sheringham in 1977, when they bought a property in Holt Road.

Prior to this Miss Evelyn Smith, leader and secretary of the Children's and Young People's Fellowship for Evangelising Britain's Villages, and her fellow worker, Miss June Wright, had been living in a wing of Baconsthorpe rectory, from where they had been working for local churches. When the rectory was put on the market finding a new home was critical. What happened next, says Evelyn, demonstrates the power of both prayer and faith. Following a national Day of Prayer the property in Holt Road became available. A loan was taken out to pay the deposit and gifts and donations enabled the purchase to be completed.

Initially, all efforts were concentrated on working with children and young people. Now the aim of the Trust is to demonstrate that the Christian message is available to everyone, regardless of belief or creed

Evelyn and her band of volunteers – 15 at the last count – feel they have established a centre where people of all faiths can come together for the

General Booth, founder of the Salvation Army.

Joy Edwards, aged 17, in Salvation Army uniform.

Robert 'Happy Bob' Farrow, a Sheringham Salvationist in the late 1880s and early 1890s, went to Grimsby to live and fish. His son, also Robert, who was a member of the J.C. Madge lifeboat crew, also went to Grimsby, where he became a member of the Spurn Head lifeboat crew.

common good – from a children's club, a monthly lunch club for the over-60s, coffee mornings and a support service for the bereaved in need of counselling or practical assistance through a troubled time. In 2009 the Trust's latest achievement has been the opening of a women's refuge in Hungary and the creation of a children's exchange scheme between local and Hungarian children.

Many Sheringham fishermen sought a new life by moving to the port of Grimsby, where most of them joined in the activities of the town's Salvation Army, singing in their choirs, helping to build a new citadel and carving a pulpit.

So enthusiastic did they become about this new (to them) form of religion that when they returned home they persuaded former colleagues and friends to adopt it.

Sadly, their early days were not happy ones, with reports of horses and traps being driven through their meetings, which they were then prohibited from holding on the promenade.

Salvation Army accordian band. Left to right, back row: *Ted Stolworthy, 'Downtide' West, Ronnie Allen*; middle row: *Phyllis Reeder, Joy Long, Clara Pegg, Vera May, Margy Blyth*; front row: *Jean Blyth, David West, Joyce Bishop.*

Sheringham fishermen were hard drinkers, and many a week's hard-earned income had all but vanished by the time the so-called breadwinner arrived home.

The 'drunk raids' made by Army girls with their copies of the *War Cry* were a familiar sight in the town in the early days, and they must have pricked a few consciences because several fishermen did admit to having been 'saved' from the perils of drink, Benny Brown being one of them.

Today the Salvation Army is an integral part of our community, respected for everything it does for the town. With an eye on the future and plans to expand their existing wide range of services, there is

a planned £1 million project to rebuild on their present site.

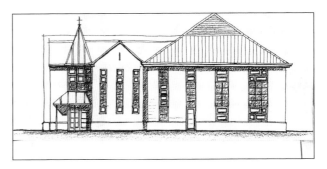

An artist's impression of the proposed new hall.

Sheringham People

Grandfather Craske, photographed by Olive and Katherine Edis.

'Old' Fiddy West.

'Old' Jimmy Mace Johnson.

Right: *Robert Gladden and Mary Maria Davison. He was coxswain of the lifeboat* William Bennett.

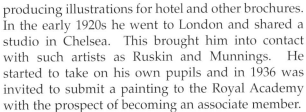

CHAPTER 6

People

Tom Armes, 1894–1963

Tom Armes was born in St Ives, Cambridgeshire, where his father was a farmer and innkeeper. From an early age he showed great potential in drawing and painting and on leaving school went to the Cambridge School of Art, where, in 1913, he was awarded a scholarship to study in The Hague. The outbreak of war in 1914 meant a hasty return home and enlistment in the Cambridgeshire Regiment followed by active service in France, a knee wound and a return home for surgery and convalescence. On discharge from hospital Tom enlisted in the Artists' Rifles. Back in the Front Line in France he suffered a second, more serious, wound which resulted in his discharge from the Army. The ensuing years were not kind to Tom. He was laid low during the 'flu epidemic of 1919, followed by a bout of tuberculosis and a lengthy convalescence period. During all this time he continued to paint and decided to become a full-time painter. At first life was hard, and Tom had to supplement his painting by taking on odd jobs such as decorating, piano tuning and producing illustrations for hotel and other brochures. In the early 1920s he went to London and shared a studio in Chelsea. This brought him into contact with such artists as Ruskin and Munnings. He started to take on his own pupils and in 1936 was invited to submit a painting to the Royal Academy with the prospect of becoming an associate member.

Ill health denied this opportunity for advancement, and following a chest operation he moved to Dorset, where he met his wife, Myra. In 1949 they came to Sheringham and settled in 'Mount Felix' in Vincent Road. Tom was soon commissioned by both the Town Council and British Railways to paint promotional posters extolling Sheringham as a holiday destination. Paintings by Tom Armes always find a ready market and are increasing in value, confirming his simple conviction, 'To paint what I see', a philosophy which he has applied to producing paintings with a purely local flavour that the public can understand and be proud to have on display in their homes.

Mick Bensley

Mick Bensley was born in Sheringham and grew up watching the fishermen working on the beach, listening to their tales and understanding the environment in which they worked. He also began to understand the many moods of the restless North Sea that provided both the source of the fishermen's

Tom Armes.

Mick Bensley.

livelihood and a watery grave if they were caught unprepared. On leaving school Mick was a student at the Norwich School of Art before working for 15 years as a graphic designer and illustrator at a leading London agency.

In 1980 he returned to Norfolk to become a full-time painter. In this author's opinion what makes Bensley's work stand apart from the work of other maritime artists is the painstaking research he undertakes to make sure that every fact and nuance of the scene he is painting is as true to life as possible. As HRH The Duke of Kent, President of the RNLI, has commented: 'Bensley's vivid paintings express the power and movement of the sea in a way that words, and even photography, are so often inadequate to convey.'

At the time of writing Mick lives and works overlooking the sea at Rottingdean on the Sussex coast.

Benny Brown

Benjamin Christopher Johnson Brown was a true Shannock whose grandfather, Ben Johnson, reputedly built all, or most, of the properties in The Avenue and Cliff Road.

Benny wanted to marry Honour Matilda Sadler but her parents did not regard him as a suitable husband for their daughter, so they sent her to stay with relatives in Grimsby, well out of Benny's reach.

They had, however, underestimated Benny's determination. He walked all the way to the Humber town and because he did not have any money to pay the toll at Long Sutton he swam the River Nene.

Somehow he brought his sweetheart back to Sheringham and they were married in All Saints Church in Upper Sheringham. It must have been a true-love match because they had seven sons and seven daughters who, on reaching school age, went to the village school, Benny paying 2d. each week for their education.

He became a fishmonger and developed a drink problem, one of his relations recalling that he developed a country round hawking fish through Sheringham's neighbouring villages. He would frequently arrive home in the trap dead drunk, but the horse fortunately knew the way home, even to the extent of being able to knock on the cottage door with its head. Benny would then be carried indoors, undressed and put to bed. He was 'saved' from his addiction to drink by the Salvation Army, which he subsequently joined, becoming a staunch supporter. He became a model citizen, was elected to the Urban District Council, which he served intelligently until his death on 2 April 1926.

As his funeral cortège moved up the High Street toward the church one of the horses pulling the hearse reared up and a potential disaster was avoided when John Craske, father of Stanley, ran out

The funeral procession of Benny Brown (top) *in some disarray, as, are members of the Salvation Army band* (above), *who were told their music was frightening the horses!*

and calmed it down. Local photographer Harry Hodges Tansley was, fortunately for us, in the crowd of onlookers and ran out to record the scene for posterity.

John Sydney Brocklesby, 1879–1955

John Brocklesby designed and built more then 50 properties in Sheringham and for the commercial development of Lifeboat Plain.

Born in Edmonton, North London, on 11 October 1879, he moved to Merton (now in the Greater London area) with his family in the early 1880s. His walk to school took him past some building sites, and it was these that sparked an early interest in building techniques and design. On several occasions. after illicit visits to such sites, he was late for school, often arriving in a dirty and dishevelled state.

This interest stayed with him, leading to a job with the Housing Section of the London County Council and the eventual founding of his own architectural practice. In 1905 he married Helen Clarke, the daughter of a Nottingham bookmaker, honeymooning at the Grand Hotel on Sheringham's seafront, though only for one night as John found the cost 'appallingly high'. They moved to another hotel or guest-house to complete their initial romantic stay in the town.

A property in Curtis Lane, built in the early 1920s and including many of Brocklesby's decorative features, including an inglenook.

Brocklesby cottages in St Austin's Grove, that on the right having been extended and its roofline altered.

Brocklesby was not a man to waste any time establishing good business contacts, even on his honeymoon. He was soon talking to a local builder by the name of Chapman, and this led to the purchase of land at West Runton, where they built several holiday cottages. Some of these were bought by people who had already purchased properties designed and built by Brocklesby in Merton Park. In such cases they were given the opportunity to buy a West Runton property for under £100.

Between 1906 and the outbreak of the First World War the Brocklesbys visited Sheringham every summer, staying at a holiday home they had bought in the town. This enabled him to supervise the building of new properties on Beeston Hill, Nelson Road, Conway Road and Hillside. The postwar years attracted more people to explore Sheringham, many of them looking for reasonably priced second holiday homes. It was this market that Brocklesby decided to satisfy. In cooperation with a local businessman, Mr Dale, he bought the larger part of Lifeboat Plain and the adjoining Gun Street. Although some properties were demolished, others on the Plain and in Gun Street were restored and made available for letting. In the space gained from demolitions Brocklesby built a holiday home for himself and a dance hall constructed almost entirely

of railway sleepers but complete with a sprung floor. The two men were also responsible for giving the town its first 'penny arcade'. It is thought that these two buildings were erected on what is now known as the Chequers car park, between the Crown Inn and the former Shannocks Hotel.

The two men also carried out extensive restoration work at the Two Lifeboats Hotel, the inglenook facing the front bar being designed by Brocklesby.

His major project in Sheringham, however, was the development of St Austin's Estate (known in 2009 as St Austin's Grove). This was partly funded by Brockleby's father-in-law, Percy Clarke, the first designs being submitted for approval in 1921. The original aim was to provide an estate of large houses for the rich and famous, but with a declining market for such properties the decision was taken to build more moderately priced houses which could be marketed as affordable and desirable holiday homes by the sea. These, too, proved difficult to sell, with Brocklesby's rustic designs and general lack of modern facilities not attracting the type of buyer they had in mind. After building just 16 properties on the estate the development was taken over by local builders Fetherstone & Pegg, the former being an associate of Brocklesby.

One of Brocklesby's most loyal employees was local man Bob Emery, with over ten years' service. Another local man, Major Dunn, hired lorries to Brocklesby, these being used to supply building materials to construction sites all over the country, and especially to Weybourne Mill, which was being restored with Bob Emery retained as a 'handyman'. Bob's wife, May, acted as cook while his father Reginald (the boatbuilder) acted as rent collector for properties in Sheringham.

Brocklesby was known as an 'Arts and Crafts' architect with an individual approach to design and construction. His speciality was to make the interiors of new houses appear to be somewhat older than they really were. Bob Emery is on record as saying:

We cut down trees, cut the bark off with draw knives, left them for a few days to dry, creosoted them and put them straight up. The house was full of 'pistol shots' for years after.

And again:

To make some of the new wood to look old we used, at Mr B's request, to go over to the meadow where the cows were, get their droppings, mould, water and creosote and then paint the mixture on with a lime brush. Then it looked very old.

With the restoration of Weybourne Mill completed in 1926, Brocklesby used it as a holiday home and a base from which he could supervise his projects in Sheringham and other sites throughout Norfolk.

John Craske

Born in Sheringham on 6 July 1881, John Craske was the third child of Edward and Hannah Craske and grandson to Nathaniel and Elizabeth 'Granny' Craske.

In those days large families were the norm. Nathaniel and Elizabeth had 12 children, Edward being the eleventh. Edward and Hannah only managed eight children and all were brought up as Salvationists, as were their grandparents.

The menfolk had been fishermen, and this was the destiny of the boys, with John spending his formative years surrounded by the fishermen characters of what was then, before the arrival of the railway, a small, introverted, parochial fishing community rarely visited by 'outsiders'.

He would have seen the arrival of the railway in June 1887, just before the family moved to Grimsby, where he went to the local board school. On leaving school he went to sea as a cabin boy.

By 1900 Edward and Hannah, with John, were back in Sheringham, but only for a brief period. In 1905 they moved to Dereham, opening a fish shop at No. 1 Wellington Road. They continued their Salvation Army activities, becoming leading members of the Dereham Corps and attending services at the Citadel in St Nicholas Street. John became a familiar figure as he stood on a box in the Market Place preaching and leading hymn singing. It was this activity that brought him to the notice of a young lady named Laura Eke – so much so that they were married in the town's Primitive Methodist Chapel on 27 July 1908.

They set up home in Swanton Morley, John establishing a country fish round. His two ponies became a familiar sight as they carried panniers of fish slung over their backs.

John Craske, fisherman and painter in wools.

Works by John Craske.

Family friends have recalled John as a tireless worker, often working 16–17 hours a day to build up his business. To make life somewhat easier they moved to North Elmham, where fish supplies from Lowestoft could be collected from the station.

By 1914 they were back in Dereham, with John continuing to cure and smoke fish both for his father's shop and his own rounds.

It is not clear whether John volunteered or was conscripted into the Army in 1914. What is known is that despite failing two medical examinations he was eventually served with his call-up papers and joined the Bedfordshire Regiment in March 1917.

This development was to prove a defining one in John's life, for within a month he contracted influenza, was diagnosed as having an abscess on the brain and was experiencing bouts of nervous collapse. His condition was so serious that he was moved to the mental wing of the then named 'War Hospital' at Thorpe, just outside Norwich.

Apparently considered incurable, he was discharged on 31 October 1918 into Laura's care with the prognosis that he was suffering from 'harmless mental stupors'. Although later diagnosed as a diabetic, this was not detected at the time of his release from hospital and one is left to imagine what this young man's future might have been had medical knowledge then been as it is today.

Sitting around the house all day did not appeal to John. He expressed a wish to go back to sea, so he and Laura journeyed up to Grimsby to stay with brother Robert. This, however, did not work out and they were both soon back in Dereham where, just before Easter 1919, they opened a fish shop at No. 15 Norwich Street. This proved highly successful and life began to look much rosier.

Within a year, however, John's father died, which had a dramatic effect on the son's health, resulting in a complete collapse and confinement to a wheelchair. On his doctor's advice they spent a spell by the sea, renting a cottage known as 'The Pightle' in Blakeney.

After a few months they returned to Dereham, and it was about this time that John started to paint. Money was short and he had to make do with any materials he could lay his hands on, with cheap household paint and whitewash key ingredients. Soon any flat surface in the house, including the back of Laura's breadboard, was covered with seascapes and pictures of boats.

This picture of the fishing boat *Gannet*, now in Sheringham Museum, is a typical example of this period of John's work, being painted on a piece of bait box! It is, nevertheless, one of his best works and one long undiscovered.

With virtually no income life was hard and the couple survived, to some extent, by introducing a form of barter in which they offered pieces of John''s work in exchange for goods and services received.

With financial help from Robert, Laura bought a small cottage at Wiveton and could almost every day be seen pushing John in his wheelchair along the coast road. They also acquired a small boat, John cutting the sail which Laura ran up on her domestic sewing machine. Trips were made to Blakeney Point and along the many creeks, and John's health slowly improved to the extent that he started to make and sell small model boats. With funds still low nails were an expensive luxury, so second-hand gramophone needles were substituted.

By early 1926 John and Laura were back in Dereham, with John helping in the family shop as and when he could.

The story is told that whilst painting one of the firm's delivery vans he suffered sunstroke. When his doctor advised a further sea cure Laura packed up house again and they moved to a cottage in Hemsby

Life here seemed to suit them, for they soon became staunch members of the Methodist Church and John was often seen driving grocer Tom Gray's horse-drawn delivery van through the village streets.

It was, moreover, this spell in Hemsby that inadvertently led to John Craske's subsequent fame as a primitive fisherman artist. He had continued his paintings and the making of model boats and one day received a visit from the artist Valentine Ackland. She wanted to buy a model boat for a friend and whilst there saw some of John's paintings. She bought one, a large representation of the fishing boat *The James Everard*, named after John and Laura's fathers; the price was £1.10s.0d. (75p).

Soon, however, the couple returned to Dereham, where John's health deteriorated. In an attempt to control his restlessness and discomfort Laura suggested he tried his hand at needlework. Somehow they managed to persuade Laura's mother to part with a piece of calico she had bought especially in which to cook her Christmas pudding, and a new talent was born.

The calico was stretched over a frame, an outline of a boat was drawn on it and Laura showed her husband the basic art of needlework. As the picture progressed the wool ran out so the sky was completed with Laura concocting a mixture of distemper and the contents of her mother's blue bag!

John quickly developed a very individual style of work he once described as 'painting in wools', using padded stitches to simulate waves and creating stunning skies equal to any in paintings by contemporary artists.

In the meantime Valentine Ackland had been asked by Dorothy Warren, owner of the Warren Galleries in Maddox Street, London, to try and get some of John's work for an exhibition in her galleries. When Valentine visited the couple, John was in a coma, but Laura let her take some of his work back to London with more, including needlework pictures, following after Dorothy herself visited the Craskes.

The exhibition was highly successful, press

reviews were good and commissions soon followed, including one for the Courtauld family yacht. A further exhibition was held in 1933 and in 1941 John was to receive international recognition when his work was exhibited at the American British Art Centre in New York.

John Craske died on 26 August 1943 in the Norfolk and Norwich Hospital from a combination of septicaemia, cervical adenitis and diabetes. At the time of his death he was working on a massive needlework picture (132 x 22ins) depicting the Evacuation of Dunkirk.

This unfinished picture is currently in the reserve collection of the Norfolk Museums and Archaeology Service in Carrow House, Norwich.

An even larger needlework 'Panorama of the Norfolk Coast' (179ins long x 16ins deep) can be seen in Glandford Shell Museum, between Letheringsett and Blakeney.

Laura, devoted wife and supporter, survived her husband by 13 years, being found dead in her kitchen by John's younger brother, James. Both rest in one grave in Dereham churchyard.

Although John's life was dogged by illness and misfortune, he is remembered by nephew Douglas, now living in South Australia, as a gentle person never known to complain of his illness.

His religion was the central factor in his life, and in Laura's, with Douglas recalling the time John told him of the prayer meetings they would hold whilst fishing, and how they followed the reflection of the moon on the sea to find the shoals of whiting. They received 2s.6d. (12½p) for a kit (140lbs) of fish.

Life may have been hard and uncertain for John and Laura, but his legacy of inspiring art is there for us to enjoy.

Stanley Craske, 1913–98

Stanley was a gem amongst colleagues. The author met him when taking up an appointment with the former Erpingham Rural District Council in 1963 and stayed through to its elimination and incorporation into the new North Norfolk District Council in 1974.

Stanley had done what very few of us do, only to repent it in later years. He talked to his parents, grandparents and relations asking them for information on their early lives – what they did, any memories they had, how Sheringham had changed, the 'characters' they knew, and what they thought of the 'modern generation'. Importantly, Stanley wrote it all down, resulting in an encyclopaedic knowledge so that when anyone came into the Council Offices and approached a member of staff with a question, however obscure, about Sheringham, the answer was always the same: 'You'd better ask Stanley.'

He was descended from the Craskes and Wests, two fishing families with Sheringham roots going back some 200 years. His father, John Gladden, was

Stanley Craske – just as we remember him.

(COURTESY ROY CRASKE)

a baker, and he numbered two lifeboat coxswains, Robert Davison (the *William Bennett*) and Obadiah Cooper (the *J.C. Madge*) among his uncles. He worked for the Erpingham RDC for 45 years except for service during the Second World War with the Royal Artillery.

Stanley married Winifred Rollins in 1935, their son, Roy, growing up to share his father's interest in local history. Stanley's mother, Ann, had been a widow for some 25 years when she moved to Sheringham in 1949 to live with Stanley. She was born in 1875 and one can only imagine the range of questions she had to answer to provide her son with new material!

Olive Edis, 1876–1955

Olive Edis was born on 3 September 1876, eldest daughter of Mary and Arthur Wellesley Edis. Her father had a medical practice in Wimpole Street, London, and held the post of Professor of Gynaecology at the London Hospital.

As she grew up she appears to have been closest to her sister Katherine, one of twins. Together they developed an interest in photography, no doubt encouraged by the work of their great-uncle, Surgeon-General John Murray, who established himself as an early pioneer of photography, making his own cameras and developing his own prints. His daughter Caroline was Olive's first 'sitter'.

In an age when women's rights and capabilities were still largely unrecognised and not openly encouraged, Olive blazed a trail of independence and professionalism that has left us a photographic archive of people, places and societies which are now relegated to history.

In their early years the sisters worked together, this continuing until October 1907, when Katherine married and moved to Scotland. Olive was never shy of approaching prospective sitters with samples of her work and the offer of a free portrait. Family connections, largely through her father's work, were obviously important. Amongst her clients were Queen Ena of Spain, Lloyd George, Bernard Shaw, Thomas Hardy, Ramsay MacDonald and her husband's cousin, John Galsworthy, author of *The Forsyte Saga*. Whilst studying at Cambridge Olive met and developed a friendship with the three princes Henry, Albert and Edward, all of whom she photographed.

Her letterheads show that she had studios in London, Farnham and Sheringham, the latter being 'discovered' by the rich and famous following the arrival of the railway in June 1887. In 1905 she opened a studio in Church Street with her sister Katherine, and many of their clients came from the notables who spent the summer season either in the town's hotels or at their large 'holiday homes', typified by one named 'The Cottage', which boasted 13 bedrooms and extensive gardens.

Olive was to spend the rest of her professional life in Sheringham, and it was here she really made her name with photographs of the local fishermen, a superb collection of black and white images which she oil painted over and which, in reproduction form, are still popular today.

As with all her portraits, she scorned the use of artificial light, together with the newly emerging primitive flash equipment. Believing a person's face to be an index of the inner character, she stated:

One is truly not a photographer unless one's work shows what is inside the sitter as well as what is outside. I have looked in secret despair at some persons who have come to my studio in Sheringham but after I studied them awhile and talked to them I have always discovered an attractive aspect. You see, there's a great deal in being in sympathy with your sitters.

She continued: '... and the photograph... should be the X-ray of the soul.'

Unlike many of today's studios, where cosmetics and retouching techniques are used to enhance the appearance of the sitter, Olive Edis would have none of this. What you saw was what you got. The wrinkles, the double chin, pimples and the long nose all stayed in, for as she said:

If a man loves a woman it is her photograph that he wants to carry about with him or keep on his desk. If all he wants is a picture of a pretty girl he can cut that out of a magazine.

You only have to look at her fishermen portraits to appreciate her work. As one reviewer put it:

Her pictures give one the impression that she has walked quietly and suddenly upon her sitters and portrayed them before they had time to assume a pose of studied expression. They breathe life and naturalness.

Olive Edis in 1914.

Olive Edis.

Women ambulance drivers photographed by Olive Edis during her tour of First World War battlefield sites in 1919.
(COURTESY THE IMPERIAL WAR MUSEUM)

Mrs Edis photographed by her daugter Olive
(COURTESY SHERINGHAM MUSEUM)

Olive and her husband, Edwin Henry Galsworthy, at their home in South Street, Sheringham.

The quality of her work was recognised in 1914, when she was admitted as a Fellow of the Royal Photographic Society. Further recognition came in March 1919 when, on behalf of the Women's Work Committee of the National War Museum (now the Imperial War Museum), she embarked on a four week, 2,000 mile tour of battlefield sites throughout France and Belgium. Her brief was to record the work of the women's services 'from a woman's point of view'. Transport was provided by the British Red Cross Society and she took with her one large field camera capable of taking large-format 10in. x 8in. plates, plus a smaller 7in. x 8in. plate camera as a safety measure. A small folding Kodak camera was included in case all else failed! Her target was to take no more than 200 prints; she ended up with 171 images.

Whereas previous war photographers had been concerned with producing images for the popular press as morale boosters, Olive's work was of a more serious nature. She was concerned that her official position as a war photographer should be recognised, this being achieved by a badge bearing the initials 'NWM' worn in her cap. She was reportedly 'amused' when asked if these stood for 'New Women's Movement'. Despite the availability of new flash equipment she refused to use it: 'I have avoided using flash exposures – and managed to get results under the most difficult conditions by daylight.'

In 1920 Olive was commissioned by the Canadian Pacific Railway to spend four months recording the scenery, industries, wildlife, people and settlements of this emerging Commonwealth country. She was provided with a specially adapted railway carriage, complete with darkrooms, bedrooms, dining-room and kitchen, together with the unusual luxury of 'real coal fires'.

Among her focused subjects were lumber camps, whaling stations, Indian communities and the natural beauty of the Rockies and Vancouver Island. Local guides and packhorses were provided to gain access to selected remote areas.

Proof that she was not the first photographer to record Indian life came when she asked Indians to pose for her. They tended to retire into their tents, the only response being a surly, 'How much you give?' and no great readiness to emerge.

As always, Olive was keen to promote her professionalism through the holding of exhibitions of her work, this being crowned by a visit by the princes Henry and Albert, Queen Mary and Princess Mary to her Canadian photographic exhibition in London.

On a more local level, when she exhibited in Sheringham in 1951 at Sadler's Picture Palace, the Norfolk Education Committee gave local children a half day's holiday to visit the show. The hall was packed with some 300 children, plus parents, on a day when the temperature was in the nineties. In addition to her photographs there was a film showing scenes of Canadian life taken by the Prince of Wales, and according to Olive all joined in 'with great gusto' to sing 'God Bless the Prince of Wales'.

In 1927 she married Edwin Henry Galsworthy, cousin of author John Galsworthy.

Olive died on 28 December 1955, aged 79, at her home at No. 32 Ladbroke Grove, London. Her body was cremated, her ashes being buried in Sheringham cemetery with her husband, who had died in Sheringham on 12 August 1947, aged 86. She bequeathed over 200 of her photographs to the National Portrait Gallery in London.

Olive Edis is remembered with great affection as a friendly personality, an incessant talker and a driver who suffered from ever-increasing car insurance premiums.

Acknowledgement is made to Sheringham Museum for the illustrations used and permission to quote from a booklet written by the author on the occasion of an exhibition of Olive Edis photographs in 1996.

Revd Charles Silvester Horne, 1865-1914

A leading Congregational minister of the late-Victorian and early-Edwardian era with a holiday home in Sheringham, Horne was educated at Glasgow University and Mansfield College, Oxford, and during the period 1889–1903 was minister of Kensington Congregational Church, then of Whitefield's Tabernacle, Tottenham Court Road, where he established a mission.

The Revd Charles Silvester Horne.

Miss Ruby Hunt in her home studio.

In 1892 he married Katharine Maria Cozens Hardy, eldest daughter of Herbert Cozens Hardy of Letheringsett Hall, who, when in London with his family, worshipped at the Kensington church.

Their holiday home was The Bluff on the East Cliff, and they paid Robert Gladden Davison and John Gladden Craske as caretakers to look after the property when they were away. Mrs Eliza Cooper, wife of Obidiah Cooper, cooked for them during their stays in Sheringham, during which times they were regular members of the congregation at Beeston Road Methodist Church. Whilst in Sheringham they probably met two members of Horne's London church, Augustine Birrell, Liberal politician and President of the Board of Education who was one of Olive Edis's sitters, and Dame Clara Butt, who regularly visited Sheringham and is on record as having sung in St Peter's Church.

Horne was elected Liberal MP for Ipswich in 1910, and whether it was the responsibilities of this job piled on top of his church work is not known, but he died at the relatively early age of 47 as he walked with his wife on the deck of a ship taking them to Canada for a planned lecture tour.

Although his book, *The Popular History of the Free Churches*, published in 1903, met with considerable success, it will be through his son Kenneth that he will be remembered, for who can forget the latter's memorable performances in such radio shows as *Beyond Our Ken* and *Round the Horne*?

Ruby Hunt, 1903–93

Ruby Hunt was born in Sheringham in 1903, daughter of Albert Hunt, purveyor of clothes, shoes, overalls, everyday and working gear for the working man from his shop just across the alleyway that sepa-

rated him from the shop of his brother Walter, nick-named 'Posh' Hunt by the locals because his upmarket clothes and shoes were priced beyond the means of the predominantly fishing community.

In her early years Ruby attended a 'little kinder-garten school' on the Cromer Road (probably Mrs Almond's). Whilst there an art teacher sparked and encouraged Ruby's interest in painting. Very soon this interest developed into a passion to the point where her desire was to go to university to further her dream of becoming a full-time painter. Unfortunately this was not to be; her father wrote to the school asking them to release his daughter because he needed her to work in his shop.

Ruby had inherited her mother's interest in the work of the Red Cross, joining it as soon as she could. Although kept busy during the inter-war years working in the shop and using her father's van to deliver and collect orders throughout Norfolk villages, she and her brother Leslie also drove the local ambulance, collecting patients and taking them to hospital and then returning them home. There is no evidence that Ruby ever passed a driving test.

Despite the demands of the shop work Ruby found time to travel throughout Britain, and squeezed in a brief tour of Northern Europe.

She enjoyed horse riding, usually on a Sunday morning, and although there is no evidence she ever owned a horse it has been suggested that one of her favourites was one of Lusher's, which normally spent the week pulling the cart used to deliver bread and cakes to customers in the surrounding villages.

Miss Alice Jefferis

Miss Alice Jefferis (her spelling) or Jeffries (press spelling) lived at 'Alwyn', later 'Oak Lodge' in Fisheram Street (now Morris Street), where she held winter wood-carving classes for young men, usually the sons of fishermen, between the ages of 12 and 16, although some documents say 12–21 years of age.

Regular exhibitions of the students' work were held, upward of 140 items being displayed, ranging

An example of work by one of Miss Jeffris's students – note the intricate carving.

from breadboards and medicine chests to inkstands and tables, walnut and oak being the principal woods used. According to one press report: 'The various articles shown reflected much credit alike to teacher and taught and it is not surprising that there is an increasing demand for the goods.' The classes were started in 1898 with just five boys, this number increasing to a maximum of 24 over the ensuing years; they were mainly from fishing families and were encouraged by the 25 per cent commission they received from every item they made which was sold. During the 1909 exhibition Mr Douglas King and his wife made some purchases, including a picture frame made by P. West, a pair of steps made by Master Barney and a hat-rack by C. Holey. A somewhat disparaging and completely unnecessary comment on the exhibition was made by Miss Dymes, Secretary of Home Arts, London, who expressed the opinion that 'considering the class of boys competing the exhibits showed a high order of skill'. A real backhanded compliment, balanced, perhaps, by a reader's letter to the local paper. Signing him or herself as a 'A visitor to Sheringham', it praised the 'extremely good' exhibition at the town's Mission Hall, with all the pieces exhibited 'reflecting great credit on the boys and their teacher'. Local press reports during the period 1908–1912 paid special attention to, and praised the work of, local lads G. Pigott, J. Scotter, J. Fennell, T. Cooper, Reginald Barcham, W. Tuck, 'Master' Barney, C. Holey, P. West and three new boys, Oiley, Silburn and Bishop.

There was a standing invitation to anyone who was interested in the work of the boys to call in to Oak Lodge, where samples of their work could be seen and orders placed.

Willie Long 1859–1946

William Long (always known as Willie) was born in Sheringham on 6 January 1859, youngest son of Robert and Martha Long. Martha was headmistress of the Infant School on the West Cliff, just to the seaward side of Mr Funnel's garage. Robert was a teacher at the school, a fisherman and a member of the *Augusta* lifeboat crew. Both parents were devout Christians and members of the Methodist Church. Willie therefore grew up and developed in a strong Christian environment, with regular daily prayers plus instruction and an understanding of the Bible and its contents.

Willie always wanted to be a fisherman and at the age of eleven he went with his father and crew on a night's fishing in the *Endeavour*. It was subsequently recorded that Willie 'went nearly mad with excitement' when the nets were hauled in, crying out 'Here comes one!' Then, 'Here comes another!" The total catch was later reported to be an incredible and almost unbelievable total of 'about twenty thousand herrings'.

On 10 October 1874 Willie went on his first long sea trip in the smack the *Welcome Home*, skippered by his brother John. The destination was Great Yarmouth, and soon after docking the crew went ashore. Within minutes two of them came back reporting colleagues were in trouble with the police. John immediately went to see what was happening only to be arrested, put in a cell overnight and taken before the magistrates the following morning. He was completely exonerated from any involvement in the 'Riot', found 'Not Guilty' and freed.

Soon after coming of age Willie went to, and settled in, Grimsby, making a living by serving as a

Willie Long, photographed by Olive Edis.

crew member on various smacks working out of the port. He later married a Sheringham girl, Mary Elizabeth Craske, and they set up home at 173 Guildford Street in Grimsby.

Before returning to Sheringham they had a daughter, Mary Elizabeth, and a son, Robert William, and brought them home by train, Willie returning to Grimsby to load their furniture and effects onto the fishing smack *The Pearl*, of which he was the skipper, and then sailing back to Sheringham. In a marriage that lasted over 60 years Willie and Mary had seven children, son Edward and daughters Dorothy, Esther, Martha and Mary Ann, known as Annie, plus the son and daughter born whilst living in Grimsby. With a background of being brought up and educated in a religious family home, Willie had always been interested in preachers and preaching, so much so that whilst living in Grimsby he started to attend revival meetings at the local Salvation Army Citadel. It was after one of these meeting that he realised he had been 'saved' and that his future lay not in being a fisherman but as a preacher, converting his fellow fishermen and others to Christianity and a belief in God. On his return to Sheringham he joined the Primitive Methodist Society and began his programme of revival to persuade ordinary people to be 'born again' in the Christian faith. It soon became clear to all that he had a gift for natural oratory, complete with a Norfolk accent and some dialect.

He was soon in great demand as a preacher and in January 1900 was invited to conduct a mission in London's St George's Hall. In order to quell his anxiety about his appearance at such a prestigious venue he asked to be allowed to take his friends, John West and Tony Craske, with him.

Perhaps it was the unusual sight of evangelists dressed as fishermen that appealed to the audience. Whatever it was it certainly worked, with drunks, ragged down-and-outs and a wide cross-section of London's poor and vulnerable following the bands and processions which attended the Hall during the ten week mission. By now Willie was in great demand, travelling throughout Norfolk and Suffolk and then by invitation to preaching engagements as far afield as Derby, Lincoln, Bury St Edmunds, Filey and several venues throughout London. On several occasions he was accompanied by his friends, John West and Tony Craske.

People in his audiences never knew he was fighting a losing battle with blindness because he knew by heart the stories and quotes from the Bible he was using; no prompting was necessary or requested. In 1934 Willie and Mary moved to a bungalow in West Runton, where Willie concentrated his efforts in raising funds both to pay off the debt outstanding on the small roadside wooden Methodist Church and to raise money to build a new one.

A year later Willie completed 50 years as a Methodist local preacher, and at a public meeting chaired by Sir Henry Upcher at the Station Road church he was presented with an illuminated address and honoured as 'the greatest preacher the church had produced'. He and Mary celebrated their diamond wedding on 28 December 1941, the service being conducted by New Zealander the Revd E.P. Blamires. Among those present were four children, 15 grandchildren and 13 great-grandchildren. Willie Long died on 1 November 1946 and is buried in West Runton churchyard. Mary died on 6 June 1949. Willie's name lives on with the new Methodist Church, known by local people more appropriately as the Willie Long Memorial Church. To them and many others William Long will always be remembered as the Fisherman Evangelist, fishing for souls with a sincerity still remembered by many Sheringham families.

Willie's story is told in a book published in 1950 and written by Herbert H. Middleton. I am grateful to Mrs Joy Edwards, one of Willie's granddaughters, for permission to use material from it in this small tribute to one of Sheringham's greatest men.

Mary Mann, 1848–1929

Mary Mann is increasingly being recognised as 'one of' the greatest talents of the late-Victorian age'. To many people her writing surpasses anything produced by Thomas Hardy, and she is accepted as a Norfolk writer in tune with the agricultural history of our county, with first-hand knowledge of living through the farming depression of the 1880s and '90s, when cheap imported foods flooded our markets.

In 1871 she married Fairman Mann, who farmed some 800 acres in and around the village of Shropham, near Attleborough. With four young children to bring up and educate and her husband's income falling, the money she made from her 32

Mrs Mary Mann.   (COURTESY KEITH SKIPPER)

novels and collections of short stories became an essential part of everyday life.

Mary helped out at the local school and spent time visiting the old, the sick and the poor, many of whom lived in dread of finishing their days in the workhouse. She was obviously a lady with observant eyes and an enquiring mind, capable of storing all these experiences as background material to be used in her writing.

Together with daughters Mary Berthalina and Margery Poppy, Mary came to Sheringham in 1916, taking up residence at 'Greenlands', Nelson Road, and staying there until her death in 1929, when her body was taken back to Shropham for burial. In 1933 her two unmarried daughters were living at 'Three Corners', Beeston Hill.

No trace has been found of Mary's life and activities during her days in the town, apart from the fact that daughter Berthalina was killed by a train as she walked over the Beeston Crossing. It was this accident that led to train drivers being instructed to sound their siren every time they approached this particular crossing.

The Larks Press has taken the initiative to reprint many of Mary's novels and short stories – recommended reading for all those who enjoy a good story with a Norfolk background and the use of dialect sensibly and not just for effect.

William Marriott.

William Marriott, 1857–1943

William Marriott was born in Basle, Switzerland, where his father was Professor of English at the local university. In the mid-1870s his name appears as a pupil engineer and then as a draughtsman at the Ipswich engineering firm of Ransomes & Rapier, designers and manufacturers of railway plant, cranes and excavators, as well as bridges and sluices. In 1988 they sold their patents and technology, but it must have been whilst with the company that Marriott developed his interest in railway construction and management. In the 1880s the company run by Wilkinson & Jarvis had contracts for two railway developments in Norfolk, one linking Great Yarmouth and North Walsham, the other to connect Fakenham and King's Lynn. Marriott was employed, initially, as the contractor's assistant, a post designed to end after a mere six months to coincide with his announced intention to move to America, where he planned to further his career. The move never materialised, and for the rest of his working life Marriott was closely involved with all aspects of railway development throughout Norfolk. His autobiography recalls many incidents, both amusing and tragic, which reveal the real man behind the professional front. It was as a result of the building of the link line between Holt and Cromer that Sheringham was connected and the former village of Lower Sheringham grew into the town we have today, the Premier Coastal Resort on the North Norfolk coast.

Following his retirement William remained in Sheringham until his death in 1943.

Gofather Pegg

Gofather Pegg was an outstanding man remembered for a variety of reasons. One writer has described him as the 'Pioneer of Sheringham's holiday trade', another as 'the most eyecatching of all the beach traders', with his distinctive red hat and the crowd of children he always seemed to attract. Yet another commented that Pegg was: '... one of the most astute businessmen I have ever encountered'. Robert Thomas Grimes Pegg was all of these and more.

Gofather grew up in a Sheringham we would not recognise. No railway, no hotels, no large houses, no modern facilities, no Lifeboat House and peopled by fiercely independent fishermen split into East and West End communities suspicious of any 'foreigners'.

Gofather was an Eastender, but with the arrival of the railway in 1887 and the discovery of Sheringham by holidaymakers, day-trippers and the rich and famous, he could see the potential income to be made from supplying services to this growing market.

He is credited with providing the first bathing tents, the first deckchairs, the first swimming lessons and the first short sea trips.

Initially he built five tents, simple structures made

with four cornerposts and small rafters covered with calico. Bell tents followed, and within a season or two he had over 60 tents for hire. The wood and iron deckchairs came from Randalls of North Walsham. It is recorded that Gofather kept his monopoly on the letting out of tents and chairs for some 15 years before any real competition appeared.

With the acquisition of a small dinghy, the *Four Sisters*, he introduced a thrilling new experience to visitors, taking them for a short sail or a row out to sea. A magazine feature informed its readers Gofather had, in fact, 32 different boats during his lifetime, 21 being pleasure craft. He also, it was said, owned and operated a 'large herring smack'.

Although Gofather was not a very good swimmer he did offer lessons, and reputedly built up a flourishing clientele. The fact that he, over the years, had saved six people from drowning did not do his reputation as a swimming instructor any harm.

One of those saved was well-known Harry Johnson, who owned both the Grand and Burlington hotels. As a young man he had gone to sea in a small boat with a friend. Diving overboard, he immediately got into difficulties. Gofather rescued him, as he did a Mr and Mrs Rounce, who were bathing near the East End breakwater when they were swept out to sea by the ebb tide.

A similar situation arose when Henry Scotter West and his son were returning from a fishing trip. Their boat was hit by a freak wave and capsized. The son managed to climb onto the upturned keel, but his father was trapped underneath. Fortunately, Gofather was close by and managed to pull him clear and take them both back to the beach. The story is also told of the day Gofather went to the beach very early when a young servant girl ran past him and straight into the incoming tide. Fearing she was trying to commit suicide he went after her and after 'a brief struggle' managed to bring her safely to the beach. It later transpired that this was just what she intended, her local boyfriend having jilted her for another local lass.

Although there is some disagreement about the origin of Gofather's nickname, it seems generally agreed it arose because when he started to talk he had difficulty in saying 'grandfather', shortening the word to something like 'g'father'. The alternative was 'Gofarther', which would certainly have been appropriate in his adult business life!

Humphrey Repton, 1752–1818

Humphrey Repton was born in 1752 in Bury St Edmunds, where his father was Collector of Excise. He was educated at grammar schools both in Bury and in Norwich. Once he had completed his education his parents wanted him to take a job in the textile industry, and at the age of 12 he was sent to Holland to learn the language and way of life. He returned to Norwich four years later and joined a fabric manufacturer. This proved to be an unhappy period for him because he really had no interest in the job, being much more interested in drawing and music.

He married Mary Clark, and during their 40 years of a happy marriage had 16 children, only five of whom survived their parents.

Humphrey's father had, in the early days of his son's marriage, set him up as a fabric merchant, but Humphrey did not really appreciate this and, through his disinterest, the business soon failed. All

Gofather Pegg, wearing his famous red hat.

Humphrey Repton from an etching by W. Hall.

Humphrey really wanted to do was live the life of a country gentleman, and to this end the growing family moved to the seventeenth-century Sustead Old Hall, where he could relax and accept the appointments of churchwarden, highways surveyor and landlord of the local inn.

It would appear that in addition to these activities he spent a lot of time sketching and painting the local landscape, including its parks and country houses.

He befriended his neighbour, William Windham of Felbrigg Hall and, following the latter's appointment as secretary to the Earl of Northington, Lord Lieutenant of Ireland, Repton went with him as his secretary on an official visit to the island.

On his return home Repton began an association with John Palmer, whose family ran a coaching business, including the Cromer and Sheringham 'Flyer'.

With no financial rewards forthcoming Humphrey soon found himself in financial difficulties and was forced to move to a smaller property at Hare Street in Essex. It was here that he made the critical decision that his future lay in becoming a landscape gardener. He was very fortunate in receiving commissions from across the country, with the owners of such estates as Holkham, Barningham, Catton, Hoveton and Honing in Norfolk seeking his advice and guidance. One of the reasons for his success was the series of Red Books in which he set out his ideas and plans for the prospective client. That for Abbot Upcher at Sheringham Hall was no exception, and on this occasion Humphrey had virtually a blank cheque for everything – the new house, an accompanying temple and the landscaping of some 800 acres. In many ways his ideas and practices followed in the footsteps of Lancelot 'Capability' Brown and completed the change from the formal gardens of the early-eighteenth century to the more picturesque and open landscapes which we still enjoy today. Indeed, it would not be an exaggeration to say that Humphrey Repton coined the term 'landscape gardener'.

Two of the suggestions in his Red Book were not fulfilled. Improvements to the village of Upper Sheringham were not completed, whilst that for the holding of coursing meetings on Sheringham beach were quietly forgotten.

Humphrey Repton collapsed and died on the morning of 24 March 1818, aged 65. Mary died on 6 April 1827, aged 78. Both, together with their fourth son, William, are buried in a small railed private plot adjacent to the south chancel door of Aylsham Church. There is also a memorial window to the family inside the church.

Allan Smethurst

Allan was born in Bury, Lancashire, on 18 November 1927, moving to Sheringham with his parents in 1929. He attended Sheringham Boys' School in Cremer Street, where he met and established a friendship with fellow classmate Des Barney. They discovered a joint interest in music and this continued through their schooldays at both the local school and at Paston Grammar School in North Walsham. Des recalls Allan's poor eyesight as a drawback to his scholarly achievements, and remembers with great affection the times he and Allan sat in a garden shed to sing the 'Top of the Pops' of their childhood days.

The late, sadly missed May Ayers has recalled seeing Allan regularly, as he often walked past her parent's house on the way to school accompanied by a younger pupil, May West, only daughter of legendary lifeboatman and fisherman Jimmy 'Paris' West. Tragically, May went blind and had to rely on a guide dog to get around. May Ayers kept in touch with Allan and in a moving letter he told her that he would never return to Sheringham; it simply would bring back too many memories for him.

Following the death of his father and the remarriage of his mother, Allan found himself in Cleethorpes. He continued to write song lyrics and probably was as surprised as everyone else when 'Hev You Gotta Loight Boy?' outsold the Beatles and he was receiving invitations to appear on such shows as 'Top of the Pops' (alongside the Rolling Stones) and the Des O'Connor Show and sharing billing with the likes of Adam Faith and Freddie and the Dreamers, a far cry from his postman days in Sheringham at a wage of around £12 a week! Allan's rise to fame and potential fortune was short lived, and it was due to something he could not control.

He was the perfect example of a shy, retiring, friendly man with a great sense of humour and imagination, but he had a fatal flaw which he could not

Allan Smethurst – the Singing Postman.

(Courtesy Keith Skipper)

85

overcome. He was terrified of appearing on stage.

The 'stars' of his generation frequently found solace in drugs. Allan found his in alcohol, and within a short space of time he was a true alcoholic, a condition not helped by the onset of arthritis, so that by 1970 he was no longer able to play his guitar.

Allan died on 22 December 2000 after spending his last 20 years as a recluse in the Brighowgate Salvation Army Centre in Grimsby. Major Christine Comely, the manager, conducted Allan's funeral service at Grimsby Crematorium on Friday, 12 January 2001. It is tempting to consider what heights in showbusiness Allan Smethurst could have achieved if it had not been for his stage fright. Nevertheless, he has bequeathed us a legacy of words and music which is still to be heard in homes and village halls in East Anglia, and for that we should be grateful.

Harry Hodges Tansley

This is a name known to all those who collect post-cards and photographs of Cromer and Sheringham,

because Harry Hodges Tansley became the real 'social' photographer of the area, filming not just family groups in his studios but going out to record activities such as fêtes and carnivals and events such as fires, floods and anything unusual or eye-catching in the areas of the two towns. During the Second World War, when it was an offence for any civilian to be seen with a camera, Harry must have obtained permission from the military authorities to operate more or less as usual. Otherwise we would not have the wonderful collection of photographs of events that took place in Cromer and Sheringham touched on in Chapter 1.

Harry was born in Lowestoft, the son of a carpenter who later became a North Sea Trinity Pilot. In his teens he was apprenticed to local photographer Thomas Boughton and whilst there he took what was to become an acclaimed photograph of local beachmen in their hut enjoying a quiet game of cards. He came to Sheringham in 1908 and established a studio in partnership with Jack Howard, also a former Boughton employee, who later moved to Ipswich. Harry's 'Burlington' studio in Sheringham

This photograph of lifeboat heroes was taken by Tansley whilst serving his apprenticeship with Broughton in Lowestoft and submitted for showing at an exhibition in Belgium. Note the nameplates of wrecked ships nailed to the ceiling. From left to right: *William Moor (75), James Burwood (76), Thomas Coleman (81), Mathew Coleman (81).*

Harry Hodges Tansley in 1936.

Harry Tansley was the town's first official Scoutmaster, joined the Special Constabulary in 1926 and was an active member of the Sheringham and Cromer Operatic and Dramatic Society. Both he and his wife were keen bowls players.

Following the death of his wife Harry moved to No. 30 Cabbell Road, Cromer, and in 1936 submitted a personal application for bankruptcy.

Other Sheringham businessmen who personally applied to be made bankrupt around that time were: Robert Henry Crowe (29 April 1940), outfitter, Co-operative Street; Wilfred Walter Hutson (23 October 1934), trading as a restaurant keeper, Church Street; Arthur Ernest Littlewood (5 December 1932) retail outfitter trading from 'Bo Peep' stores in Beeston Road; William John Shilton (4 November 1935) 'of no occupation' but living at Beechwood, Beeston Regis Woods; David John Williams (7 May 1935) trading as a coal merchant and general store keeper, Cooperative Street.

The following nationally known people have either stayed in hotels whilst on holiday in Sheringham or have had a holiday home in the town:

Augustine Birrell, Liberal politician, Secretary of State for Ireland

Dame Clara Butt, one of the greatest contraltos, sang in St Peter's Church

Stanley Christopherson, President of the MCC, former captain of the England cricket team

Winston Churchill, Prime Minister, stayed at the Sheringham Hotel

Ben Davies, Welsh tenor

Sir Ernest Fulton, Recorder of London

Leslie Henson, star of stage and concerts

Revd C. Silvester Horne, preacher and hymn writer

Clarkson Rose (Twinkle), star of seaside concert parties, probably appeared at Arcade Lawn open-air theatre, Church Street

Lord Justice Scrutton, Chief Justice of England

Sir Ernest Shackleton, explorer, stayed at 'Mainsail Haul', the Boulevard

J.H. Taylor, a great golfer, designed the layout of the golf course

Joyce Wethered, lady golfer, played at Sheringham golf course.

Sir Arthur Conan Doyle played golf on Sheringham course (as did a Mr Moriarty!)

was on the top floor of the building now occupied by Westcliff Gallery on the corner of Church Street and Augusta Street. In those days the ground floor was the site of a working men's club, and there are recorded occasions of them complaining to Tansley that chemicals used in his photographic business were dripping from the ceiling and spoiling the baize on the billiard tables underneath!

Harry was a familiar sight as he travelled round the area on his Douglas motorcycle and sidecar. In April 1949 he celebrated 50 years as a photographer, it being estimated that at that time his Sheringham studio housed some 30,000 negatives, with a further 24,000 in his Cromer premises.

Sheringham People

Jack Barker, local market gardener, selling his wares around Sheringham ably assisted by Fred Springall, one-time street sweeper for Sheringham UDC.

Delivering coal for 'Cutty' West are Bussy Hannah (on cart) and Joe Hall.

Sheringham People

Tom 'Crackpot' Craske. The words 'Fish Daler' (sic) were painted on the side of his cart by 'Kronjer' Pegg.

Harry Ward kept bees and sold honey from his home at Mill Cottage on the 'top' road, otherwise known as the A148 Cromer to Holt road.

Sheringham People

George 'Corgi' Craske with grandson Sydney Craske.

Robert 'Bumshee' West and wife Maria.

Henry 'Shotail' Smith West and wife Martha Ann.

John 'Teapot' West.

Right: Willam and Mary Long and grandchild.

Sheringham People

Robert and Mary Johnson.

Charlie 'Frog' Woodhouse, c.1905. At this time many properties in Sheringham relied on pail closets as their only form of sanitation. Charlie was one of a small team of 'night soil' collectors who came round weekly to provide this valuable service. The euphemistically called 'honey carts' would have been a familiar sight to late-night revellers.

Katherine Cozens Hardy, daughter of Lord Cozens Hardy, Master of the Rolls and wife of Revd Charles Silvester Horne.

William Reginald Tuck, c.1945–46.

Sheringham People

Left to right, back row: ?, ?, ?, *Amelia Grice, Elizabeth Grice;* front row: *Ann Scotter and family, with Harry Grice holding William and Hannah Grice holding Florence.*

Sheringham Gas & Water Co. employees, c.1905. Left to right, back row: Sam Smith, Albert Dyball, Sidney Dyball; second row: Stephen Purdy, Harry Dyball; front row: Charles 'Swonky' Dyball, William Crowe, Edward Craske, George Judd (Manager), Billy Craske, Charles Duffield.

Sheringham People

Staff at the Voluntary Aid Detachment Auxiliary Hospital, Vincent Road, Sheringham, March 1918.

Members of Cyril Getliffe's Ladies' Choir, who gave concerts at the Town Hall. The building later became the Little Theatre.

Sheringham Salvation Army soloists, 1914. Left to right: Edward Long, Ted Stolworthy, Eddie Blyth, John Grimes

Billy Lambert and Bob Hall ready to deliver the daily bread.

Sheringham People

An early Rolls-Royce used by Herbert Thompson. Left to right: the chauffeur, Mr Thompson's assistant, Mrs Forsdick (née Johnson), Herbert Thompson, John Robert Johnson.

The Charles Grand Orchestra. Left to right, back row: Ron Ditcham, Charles Grand (conductor), Ralph Nurse, Ted Middleton; middle row: Bob Brettingham, Hubert Middleton, ?, Billy Middleton, Bob Middleton, Eric Nurse; front row: Miss Ryde, Janet Greenly, Ruby Grand, Claire Hall, Gladys Brettingham.

Sheringham People

Above, left to right: *George Emery, Miss Fuller, Miss Barnes, Arthur Woodrow, c.1930.*

Left: *Staff of Leeder's Bakery, c.1920.*

Pupils of Crosby House School, South Street, c.1925. Left to right, back row: Joyce Blyth, Elsie Farrow, Doreen Hunt, ? Miller, Mollie West; middle row: Gladys Shypley, ? Miller, ? Miller, Joan Brett, Ivor Lewitt; front row: Charlie Payne, Alistre Kemp, Runton boy, Robert Gilbert, J. Payne, ? Miller, ? Miller.

Sheringham People

Horses and traps for hire. Left to right: *Billy Sayer, Joe Hall, ?.*

At work in the railway goods yard. Left to right, on cart: *Kiff Pegg, Donny Hannah, Cutty West, D.D. Hannah (holding the horse);* front row: *John Cox, Bussey Hannah, Croake Sadler.*

Sheringham People

Rebuilding the Crown Inn, 1935–37. The contract was given to T. Gill & Son (Norwich) Ltd – Sidney Gill can be seen on the far right and his foreman on the far left. While some of the workmen were brought down from Norwich, many local men were also employed, including Roger, Chris and Harold Emery, who are all in the middle row. The photograph was taken by a passing beach photographer. (COURTESY MR ANDREW GILL)

Sheringham firemen at the Grand Hotel, c.1938/39. Left to right: Alfred Draycott, Tom Starling, Basil Blyth, Jack Dyball, Harry Dyball, Tom Gray, Victor Cooper, Eddie Blyth.

Sheringham People

The Rainbow Band at 'Kingsley', Priory Road c.1934. Left to right, back row: Kathleen Grice, Margaret Grice, Joyce Bishop, Audrey Bishop, Betty Bouttell; front row: Joan Sadler, Daphne Catchpole, a Salvation Army officer's daughter. All were pupils of Mrs Ruby Nurse (née Grand)

Travellers' Rest outing, c.1946, including ? Tuck, Ernie Blyth, Stuart Taylor, Jimmy High, Donny Hannah, 'Old' Abraham Cooper, ? Gant, 'Gayton' Cooper, Downtide West, Croak Sadler, Harry Rix, William Todd, Bob Rushmer and Harry Grice. The party would meet at Salisbury House, Salisbury Road before boarding their bus.

Sheringham People

Sheringham firemen. Left to right: W. Callow, Leslie Piggott, Paddy Richardson, Alfred Draycott, ? Garrod, H Osborne, Bob Anderson, Tom Gray, Dick Broughton, Jack Dyball, Jack Brown.

Members of the Cromer and Sheringham Brass Band. Left to right: Peter Tomlinson, Bob Palmer, Henry Grice, Ted Watts (Secretary), Derek Little.

Sheringham People

A party on Beeston Common celebrating the coronation of Queen Elizabeth II in 1953. (COURTESY MRS A.M. THIRTLE)

On 14 October 1958 Wilfred Pickles visited Sheringham to record an episode of the BBC radio programme 'Have a Go' at the Secondary Modern School (the High School). Left to right: Mrs Lilly Mason, Mrs B. Rackham, Tom Cooper, Mrs Gabrielle Rees, Stanley Craske, Wilfred Pickles, Mrs A. West, Miss Brenda Wright.

Sheringham People

Henry 'Joyful' West meets the queen during her walka-bout at County Hall, Norwich, as part of her silver jubilee celebrations, 11 July 1977.

Brian Pegg at the Albert Hall, London, during the initiative 'Hi Neighbours', discussing what volunteer lifeboatmen did in their working life.

The opening of the Gazebo, Sheringham Park, 20 March 1988. Left to right: Keith Zealand (Head Warden, Sheringham Park), two helicoper crewmen, Prince Charles, Merlin Waterson (the National Trust), Bob Rushmer and a representative from the Manpower Services Agency.

Sheringham High Street, 1916.

✦ CHAPTER 7 ✦

Business and Industry

Shopping and Shops

One of the pleasures of living in Sheringham is our wide range of independent, friendly family shops. Whilst we have national representatives such as Stead & Simpson and the Co-op, plus two small supermarkets and two small off-licences, it is to the independents we go to for all basic foods such as bread, fish, meat and fresh vegetables. There is, moreover, one business which has attained 'institution' status.

Charles Arthur Sadler founded his ironmongery business in Station Road in 1897 as a means of obtaining trade discounts from his suppliers, which soon included his growing building business. This included a contract to build the new Parish Church of St Peter's at a cost of £8,000 – a fraction of the cost incurred when it was later redecorated.

Charles Arthur was joined by Horatio John Blyth, who became both general and funeral

Sadler's staff with, left to right: *Richard Wright, George Balls, Colin Voellner, Ann Willison, Ron Wright, Ivan Allison and Ivor Town.*

Sadler's store, with, left to right: *Mr Nurse, Robert 'Tintack' Forby and Horatio Blyth.*

Left to right: Clarence Wright, Sam Lubbock, Charles Postle.

Watts's stationery store and library, c.1918.

manager, and they later took on Clarence Granville Wright, who, at the age of 14, received his indentures on 25 May 1915.

When Sadler retired he offered Blyth and young Wright the opportunity to take over, and so the business as we know it today was born. Ron Wright joined the business when he was 13 and has been there ever since. Brother Richard joined soon afterwards on his return from active service in the RAF during the Second World War. He has since retired and Ron, accompanied by sons Christopher and Jamie, has built the business into what is acknowledged to be the best independent family-run ironmongers in East Anglia, attracting customers from throughout the county.

Its greatest asset is the unfailingly friendly and helpful staff, who are always willing to serve, even if this means selling you something better and cheaper than what you originally had in mind.

Bertram Adam Watts left London and arrived in Sheringham in the late 1890s, just in time to see the last undeveloped building plot in Church Street coming up for sale. It was bought to provide the town with a new Post Office, and Bertram successfully applied to rent some space on the ground floor so that he could open a small shop selling such essential items as buckets and spades, toy yachts, books, newspapers and stationery. As Sheringham grew, so

Bertram Adam Watts, 1870–1951.

B.A. Watts, Church Street.

A converted American Jeep used for paraffin deliveries.

did Bertram's range of goods, it becoming clear that the shop's success in the coming years would be based on stocking and selling a wide choice of books. By the 1930s this had been achieved, thereby laying the foundation of today's success, when the name 'Watts' is synonymous with a bookshop that is one of the best of its kind in the whole region.

Both Albert and his son Bertram, were active members of the Booksellers' Association, and in 1948 they organised the first AGM of the Association to be held outside London. The Sheringham Hotel was the official base for meetings, seminars and lectures, as well as providing accommodation for officers of the Association. It proved to be one of the most successful meetings the Association had ever had, with compliments and praise being heaped on Bertram and his staff.

On Albert's death in 1951 Bertram Albert took over the reins, continuing until his retirement in 2000. During his stewardship Bertram became involved in many aspects of local life, scoutmaster being just one of them. At the time of writing the business is run by Bertram's daughter, Catherine, and husband, Peter Hill, who are continuing the family's friendly, first-class service backed by a friendly and welcoming staff dedicated to helping with any enquiry.

Walter Starling, grandfather to David Starling, started his business career in Weybourne with a small shop and a horse and cart delivery service to neighbouring villages.

He came to Sheringham in 1895 and entered into partnership with Charles Clarke in a grocery business in Windham Street. When, a few years later, the partnership ended, Clarke opened his own grocery shop in Beeston Road. In November 1912 Walter bought a newsagent's and stationery business in the High Street, but it was not until 1973 that this was expanded into the adjoining shop.

Two former Second World War Army huts from Weybourne Camp were bought and erected at the back of the shop; they were converted into a lecture hall complete with a stage which was used regularly by members of the Primitive Methodist Church in

Station Road to stage plays under the guiding hands of Mrs Sibson. At election time it was used as a polling station for the town's central ward.

During the Christmas season the shop was known as Sheringham Bazaar, the highlight being the fancy dress parade through the town, many children arriving in charabancs from surrounding villages to see Father Christmas and compete for the solid gold half sovereign for the best costume. Despite popular support attendance was severely affected when Woolworth's and the Salvation Army opened their own grottos for their Father Christmases, and after a few years the parade was cancelled. Walter's son, also Walter, joined the business after leaving school, duly married Peggy Abbs and, following the death of his mother, bought the business from the family.

Prior to service as a dental assistant in the Army during the Second World War son David had worked for five years at Jarrold's in Norwich learning the trade of newsagency and toy retailing, and when his father retired in 1967 he and his wife, Rita, bought the business from him.

Following inspections by architect John Fetherstone and Bob Lord, it was realised that parts of the premises were showing signs of serious structural disrepair. A two-year renovation programme was put in hand and the new shop was given a right royal opening on 23 June 1973, when Pearly King Mark Tongue and his wife Queen Shirley declared it well and truly open.

In 1974 a new warehouse was built over the toy department. Barry came into the business in 1974 and in 2009 Starling's is truly a family company, with directors David, Barry and Johnathan and other members of the family managing the Holt shop, which specialises in sporting gear and equipment. There are also other branches in Dereham and Bury St Edmunds.

At the time of writing David Starling has a relatively new role as Sheringham's Post Master, a position he has held since the Post Office opened in the Sheringham shop in 1994.

If you had been in Sheringham in the mid to late 1950s and asked for directions to Hunt's shop, you would have been answered by another question – 'Which one do you want, Albert's or 'Posh' Hunt's?'. Walter Hunt and his wife, Caroline Jane, came to Sheringham in March 1892, Walter taking up the position of general manager for an outfitter's shop run by the Ransome family situated in the High Street opposite the Town Clock.

Both of them had worked in Walter's father's drapery and bootmaker's shops in London's fashionable Clarendon Place, just off Portland Road in Holland Park. When the opportunity arose in 1899 to acquire the Ransome business Walter and Caroline did not hesitate, believing that the arrival of the railway in June 1887 would be the catalyst to trans-

Wilfred and Claude Hunt outside the family shop.

Claude Hunt.

Wildred Hunt.

form the previously inward-looking fishing village into a bigger and better community. They were not to be disappointed. Public services such as gas, water and electricity, accompanied by new and improved streets and roads and the building of a new promenade, soon followed, as did new hotels amid a frenzy of building.

Walter and Caroline had the foresight to realise that the wealthy people moving into the town from London and other cities were all potential customers, and soon their shop was stocked with nationally known and exclusive brands of clothing and footwear. With trade booming space was becoming something of a problem. In 1936 they made the decision to provide a complete new shop front and extend the shop to the rear by converting former farm stables and buildings at the back which had once been part of Manor Farm. Sons Claud and Wilfred suggested creating an arcade effect using a marble floor to enhance the overall appearance. This was achieved by importing Travertine marble from Abyssinia (now Ethiopia).

At the same time as Claud and Wilfred were building up a reputation for quality clothing and footwear in one of the largest and most progressive outfitter's shops in the area, Walter's brother, Albert, was establishing himself just across the alleyway separating the brothers, as the supplier of clothing, footwear and general household items for the working man and his family. It was not long before local residents coined the phrase 'Posh' Hunts to differentiate between the two shops.

Walter's sons, Peter and David, inherited the shop, the former having gained experience of the trade working for several years for Austin Reed in London and had represented the company in their shop aboard the liner *Queen Mary* on two voyages to America.

When I asked Peter the secret of his family's successful trading his reply was brief and to the point: 'Take a pride in what you do, employ a friendly and helpful staff and provide a personal service aimed at satisfying customers who will come back again, and again.'

With retirement looming, Hunt's shop was closed in March 2005, the ground floor later being occupied by BetFreds betting shop with private flats on the first and second floors. Albert's shop closed in the late 1950s.

When you meet an acquaintance from a town some 26 miles away it is perfectly natural to say, 'Hello, what are you doing here?'. This particular answer was direct and to the point:

Oh, I usually come here most Saturdays to catch up on the shopping... We don't have an ironmongers like you have here, and mealtimes wouldn't be the same without fish from the shop behind you.

John Long with his granddaughter Annie outside what is now Scotter's shop, Station Road.

The 'shop behind' was Peter Scotter's fish shop. Peter was a fisherman, and when he 'retired' he generously donated his boat, the *Windsor Rose*, to Sheringham Museum, where it can now be seen.

Before the Scotter family interest the shop was owned and run by John Long, so this is a shop with a 40-year plus record of being involved in the same trade – something it shares with others whose histories are outlined in this book.

Renowned for the quality of its bread and cakes, Lusher's Bakery was founded in 1898 by William James Lusher on the corner of High Street and Wyndham Street on the site of the old town well known as The Polk.

The business also included seed and corn sales, all deliveries being made by horse and cart, a common sight throughout the suburbs of Sheringham and in the nearby villages of Bodham, West Beckham and Upper Sheringham. The horses were stabled in Co-operative Street, next to what was then Dave's fish and chip shop. Billy Lusher ran the cake-making side of the business, operating from new premises on the former stable site. The large ovens were originally heated by burning bundles of sticks bound together, then by coke and finally, when the shop was rebuilt in 1970, by oil.

In 1985 great-grandson Tony followed in the steps of his father and grandfather. He could see changes taking place in retailing in Sheringham, with new shops opening toward the top end of Station Road.

He took over a lock-up shop, No. 37 Station Road, on the corner of that road with Melbourne Road, this proving to be a very successful move.

Tony died in 1998 and the business was transferred to his wife, Barbara, who ran the shops and bakery until finally closing them down on Christmas Eve 1999, as she could no longer compete against supermarket prices.

Lusher's bakery business had a thriving country round. This photograph was taken in Bodham, c.1928, and shows Fred Lusher in the driving seat and William Lusher at the rear of the cart

Bread, cakes, hay and corn for sale, serving Sheringham for over 100 years and His Majesty the King for slightly less time!

Foxes, Furs and Fashions

During the 1920s and '30s no lady with any sense of fashion would have been seen at a social event of any note without her fur coat or stole, the latter complete with head, legs, feet and claws, the head being attached by a clip to her coat, jacket or dress.

Canadian trappers had long been trapping wild foxes and other fur-bearing animals and selling their pelts. In 1872 a Canadian entrepreneur, Benjamin Heywood, obtained several litters of silver foxes and tried to breed them at his base on Prince Edward Island, the smallest province of Canada in the Gulf of the St Lawrence River. He was unsuccessful, and it was not until 1895 that two men, Charles Dalton (later to become a millionaire and knighted for his services to agriculture) and Robert Oulton, both living on the island near the town of Tignish, successfully introduced a new breed of fox with a vein of silver in its fur. So popular did this become that by the end of the century Prince Edward Island had become the world centre for silver fox pelts. Other countries quickly developed their own farms, Scotland boasting the first in the UK in 1921. Within a very few years there were over 100 silver fox farms across England, Scotland and Wales.

One of the biggest and most progressive was in Sheringham, at Sheringwood, where a retired Burmese District Commissioner, James Arthur Penrhyn Stuart, bought land from Miss Ida Trotter and Miss Mona Blanche Murray during 1928 and 1929 to develop his own farm with 28 staff and 150 pairs of breeding silver foxes.

Like many of his contemporaries, he could see a new future opening up for himself and his growing family and would, no doubt, have been influenced by editorials and features in financial and investment publications and magazines such as that published by the Norwich Union.

One contributor was moved to write:

There is so much pure joy in silver fox farming, quite apart from its attractive monetary aspect. It is this joy which makes the silver fox farmer so much in love with the job he has made his own.

From the author's research it would appear that the majority of early farm owners tended to be ex-colonial Army officers, policemen and administrators who invested their savings and pensions in what was seen as a quick money-making industry.

Initially there were doubts as to whether our climate was suitable for fox farming. These, however, were soon dispelled. The coldest months in Canada at that time came in the New Year, with fox cubs emerging from their dens into the snow, rain and winds of what has been described as the 'more vigorous' Canadian spring, as opposed to the warm weather of our late spring.

At this time Stuart's letter and business heading was 'Sheringham Silver Fox Farm', with its 'Regis' Farm Quality advertising motto stating he was a

What the fashion-conscious lady would have worn in the 1920s and 1930s.

James Arthur Penrhyn Stuart.

Beeston Regis Silver Fox Farm staff. Left to right, back row: *Walter Brown, James Pegg, John Burrows, Henry Cooper, Doris Cooper, Joseph Pegg, John Murdock, James Stewart, Mrs Stewart, Mrs Goodyear, Silky Crask, Mr Titomas, Mr Dawson, Mr Earl, Dick Broughton, Jimmy Goodyear;* front row: *Ernest Pegg, Charlie Grice, Hilary Pigott, Victory Barrows, George White, Oliver Shifko, James Middleton, Bennet Middleton, Charlie Fields, Charlie Grice senr, Fred Bilham.*

Offices and reception area of the Hilltop Outdoor Centre.

The breeding pens, each of which measured 30ft x 15ft, while the cub pens measured 20ft x 10ft. Each pen was raised 10in. off the ground with access via a ramp at the front.

producer of pelts supplying live animals to both individuals and other breeders. Other farms within the county were both breeders and suppliers of fur coats, stoles and other fur accessories, potential customers being given the opportunity of visiting the breeding pens to choose which particular animals had the shade and quality of fur they wanted to order. At these farms the foxes were usually killed by chloroform gas, the pelts being sent away for curing and making up into whatever garment or accessory had been ordered. To be absolutely in fashion, stoles would be supplied as the animal's whole body, designed to drape round the shoulders with a clip so it could be fastened to the wearer's outside clothing.

James Stuart is on record as saying he confiden-

Doris Louisa Pegg, 1933.

Lions Adam and Eve.

Mr and Mrs Stuart, he with a silver fox and she with a black ape.

Peter the pelican.

tially expected the number of silver fox farms in England to rise to somewhere between 500 and 1,000 as the demand for fur continued. He pointed out that even in the depths of America's Great Depression (1929–34), when so many companies either closed down or went into bankruptcy, good-quality pelts were still fetching £25–£50 each. With production costs as low as £5–£8 per pelt, he was confident the good times would continue for silver fox farmers. With a good breeding pair of cubs fetching £125 and an adult breeding pair which had already one or more litters selling for £150 or more, it was even suggested that silver fox farming might be added to the list of careers recommended to school leavers and to women looking for a self-employed role in agriculture.

Doris Louisa Bohannan (née Pegg), 20 years old in 1932, lived in Hebron House in Nuttals Meadow on Beeston Common, from where she used to walk through Spring Wood to the silver fox farm where she had a temporary summer job as a general help for the welcome sum of 12s. a week. She remembered a driveway along the side of the Stuarts's bungalow which led down to the office and kitchen, where food for the foxes was prepared. She recalled that the kitchens were always spotlessly clean, the animals' food consisting mainly of eggs and baby turkeys: 'I had to feed the baby turkeys with crushed stinging nettles which I had gathered from around the farm.'

She remembered, too, that both the floors and the sides of the fox pens were made of chicken wire. 'They were beautiful creatures with black and silver fur,' she recalled. She also remembered a Canadian connection in that an employee from that country,

SHERINGHAM ZOO

—AND—

Silver Fox Farm

Proprietors : J. A. P. Stuart., F.Z.S.
A. Master., C.I.E.

GUIDE 3d.

OPEN EVERY DAY 10 a.m.

An advertisement for the zoo from 1934.

A somewhat apprehensive Miss Elsie Cooper from Aylmerton feeding Maisie.

Snakes alive! Rather him than me...

Surrounded by silver fox pelts.

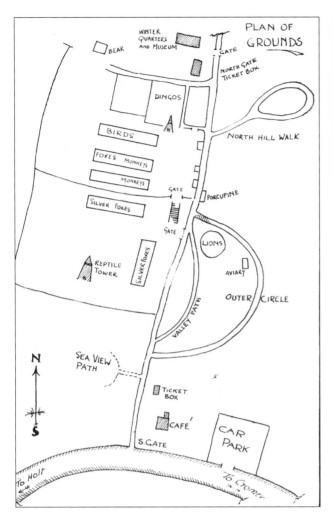

A plan of the zoo.

The farm watch tower, primarily used for recording mating pairs.

employed by the Stuarts to look after the foxes, who lived in a small cottage on the common somewhere close to Briton's Lane.

With a worldwide overproduction of fox furs and accessories business became increasingly competitive for breeders and manufacturers, and it is suspected that this may have been the reason for Mr Stuart's decision to extend his fox farm to include a zoo, which opened on 1 July 1933. A guide costing just 3d. listed 30 species of animals on display, from lions to rabbits, bears to tortoises.

The zoo café offered teas at a shilling each and à la carte lunches, plus stalls where visitors could buy fruit, biscuits, chocolate, minerals and cigarettes, as well as food suitable for feeding to the animals. Interestingly, all the animals were for sale, including Japanese foxes and racoon dogs, credited with mystical powers and thought to be the only specimens in this country.

Two mysteries remain from this fascinating era of Sheringham's history. Where did the foxes and zoo animals go when the site closed prior to the outbreak of the Second World War?

The foxes, presumably, were sold to other breeders and manufacturers. The author has been told that all the zoo animals were sent to Margate Zoo, but enquiries there have drawn a complete blank. Similarly, approaches to Regent Park Zoo in London have been completely unproductive.

At the time of writing the sites of the fox farm and zoo are occupied by the Hilltop Outdoor Centre, providing adventure and education for children and corporate entertainment and team development courses for companies. The company takes great pride in that, having started from scratch, it is now regarded as one of the best privately owned centres of its kind in the east of England and is busy all year round. Having said this, proprietor Martin Read is also proud of the history of the site they occupy, and is always pleased to welcome groups to show them reminders of the days when silver foxes were reared and the zoo was a major local attraction. Hexagonal stone water tanks can be found in the grounds, as can the foundations of the zoo kitchen and the sites of the lion cage, the snake house and sea view walks.

Sheringham Paper Mill, 1788–1861

Original research by May Ayers, Hazel Makins and Stanley Craske revealed there was a small working paper-mill in what is now Beeston Road but was then called Mill Lane and, later, Paper Mill Road. The actual site of the mill and three accompanying cottages was an area of land situated between the present Priory Road and The Avenue. It was powered by a water wheel turned by the flow of

A drawing of Sheringham paper-mill, c.1800.

water in what we now know as Beeston Beck, which must have been considerably wider then, with a stronger flow than the small rivulet we now have.

Records show that in 1788 the mill was owned by Mr Valentine Blyth, who made generous gifts to the poor of Sheringham and whose daughter married into one of the Craske families in the town.

In 1792 the mill was occupied by a Mr Bond, reverting to Valentine Blyth in 1797. The reason for his temporary absence appears to have been due to his taking up the duties of Overseer of the Poor. Also in 1797 a Mr Critoph was listed as the mill owner. He probably died fairly soon afterwards, for in 1808 the owner is listed as Mrs Critoph.

In 1851 the Census return lists the mill's owner as Sarah Skipper, residents including her son-in-law, Charles Clarke from Taverham, his wife Ann and their two children, Caroline and William.

By 1861 Charles Clarke was apparently the owner of the mill, its title having been transferred to him by his mother-in-law. His family were still living there.

The 1871 Census makes no mention of either the mill or its occupants.

The three researchers also mention the presence of a windmill at the corner of the present Beeston and Cromer roads on the site of the recreation ground. It was thought this could have been a corn-mill, the base of which could be seen until the late 1880s.

The North Norfolk Railway – The Poppy Line

The Eastern & Midlands Railway started operating on 16 June 1887 with its Melton Constable to Cromer branch line, including stops at Holt, Weybourne and Sheringham. The decision not to operate a line between Holt and Blakeney was purely a commercial one based on what the company saw as a potentially lucrative holiday trade, with visitors heading for the coast in the growing resorts of Cromer and Sheringham. On 1 July 1893 the Eastern & Midlands Railway was amalgamated with other railways in East Anglia to form the Midland & Great Northern Joint Railway, known locally as the 'Muddle & Get Nowhere Railway'. The year 1923 saw a major reorganisation of all our railway companies, one of the new names emerging being the London & North Eastern Railway (LNER), translated by the locals as the 'Late Never Early Railway'.

The nationalisation of the railways in 1948 resulted in the former M&GN lines, now owned by the LNER, becoming part of British Railways.

In 1984 the infamous Beeching cuts resulted in the Melton Constable to Sheringham line being closed, the only part of the M&GN service to survive being the Sheringham to Cromer connection. This now forms part of the very successful National Express Bittern Line from Norwich, with local organisations and groups given the opportunity to have an input into the line's management and promotion.

British Rail continued to use Sheringham Station until the spring of 1967, when they built a halt on the Cromer side of the former level crossing at the top of Station Road. A combination of local and national steam-train enthusiasts were determined to preserve Sheringham's steam-train heritage and formed Central Norfolk Enterprises Ltd, changing the name in 1969 to the North Norfolk Railway Co.

This new company is a classic example of what dedicated volunteers can achieve. They relaid the track through to Holt, where they created a new station. Workshops at Weybourne have seen engines and carriages rebuilt and refurnished. The station at Sheringham has been similarly treated and today is the kind of facility you would have experienced back in the 1920s and '30s. In 2001 the future of Sheringham Station and of the whole line was faced with the real threat of extinction when the landlords threatened to evict the railway and redevelop the site as a supermarket. Fortunately, a high-profile campaign was successful in raising enough money not only to buy the site but to carry out a full restoration programme on the station itself.

Since then the management have toiled unceasingly to implement a continual programme of improvements, resulting in the winning of such awards as 'Heritage Railway of the Year' in 2005 and coming runners-up in 'Best Visitor Attraction' and 'Outstanding Contribution to Tourism'.

The North Norfolk Railway is, however, much more than just a railway. It also organises such events as an annual 1940s weekend, a beer festival, evacuee days, Santa specials, Christmas carol concerts and gala days

One three-day gala event attracted some 10,000 visitors, many of them, especially the youngsters, experiencing their first ride in a train pulled by a steam engine.

The railway has also proved popular with television and film companies, appearing in 'Dad's Army', 'Hi-Di-Hi', 'Miss Marple', 'Swallows and Amazons', 'All the King's Men' and 'The Lost Prince'.

Another milestone in the development of the railway was the approval given by Her Majesty's Railway Inspectorate to the reinstatement of the former railway crossing at the top of Station Road.

This provides a connection to the main railway network, and whilst not intended to be used for fare-paying passenger services, it allows NNR, on an average of up to 12 occasions a year, to bring in new engines and rolling stock, the former perhaps including such favourites as the *Flying Scotsman* and the *Oliver Cromwell*, previously on display at the Bressingham steam collection.

Increased visitor numbers and the confirmation of Sheringham as a heritage centre of steam railway will enhance the North Norfolk Railway's position as the town's premier tourist attraction, with 120,000 visitors a year. In the long term the crossing could become a vital element in the development of a suggested Norfolk Orbital Railway, providing a circular railway through Norfolk run on a commercial basis and open to everyone.

The subtitle 'Poppy Line' is based on Victorian writer Clement Scott's features in the *Daily Telegraph* in which he eulogised the attractive countryside, attractions and people in the Cromer and Overstrand areas with special mention of the latter village's Garden of Sleep on the cliff top.

A World First Service for Sheringham

In 1948 the Royal Mail started a series of experimental helicopter mail deliveries, East Anglia being identified as the region in the whole of the country 'most in need of acceleration'.

Trial flights started that June using 'live' mail for a trial period of three months, with Peterborough and Great Yarmouth as the two terminals.

Initially two flights a day were planned, the morning one starting from Peterborough with mail drops at King's Lynn, Wells, Sheringham, Cromer, Norwich, Thetford, Diss, Harleston and Great Yarmouth. An evening service from Great Yarmouth picked up mail there and then at Lowestoft, Beccles, Norwich and Dereham before returning direct to Peterborough. Significantly, there was no extra postage to pay for this service, with many of the letters and packages carrying the 2½d. Royal Wedding stamp.

At Sheringham the landing ground was the recreation ground on the Holt Road, it being claimed that a letter posted in Peterborough by 9a.m. could be delivered in Sheringham by midday. By September over 30,000lbs of mail had been successfully dropped

The first flight of mail to Sheringham.

First-day cover celebrating the inaugural flight of the Peterborough–Norwich–Great Yarmouth service.

off, 95 per cent of the flights being safely completed. During February and March 1949 experimental night flights between Peterborough and Norwich were successfully completed, as a result of which the Post Office awarded a six-month contract to British European Airways Helicopter Unit to run a night service between Peterborough and Norwich; it took just 45 minutes to complete the 67 miles between the two terminals.

The Sheringham Shoal Offshore Windfarm

At the time of writing the government has approved an application by Scira Offshore Energy Ltd to develop a windfarm 10–15 miles due north of Sheringham. Work has already started on the project which, by the end of 2011, will see this £750 million investment providing power to some 210,000 homes.

The diamond-shaped site will contain 88 turbines, each 260ft tall. They will be connected to a network of marine cables linked to offshore transformer stations within the windfarm before other marine cables bring the energy ashore at Weybourne. From here underground cables will feed the electricity to an existing, as well as a proposed new, electricity substation at Salle, near Cawston. The site of the windfarm was chosen because it experiences high wind speeds, has relatively low levels of fishing activity, is within a government approved area for redevelopment and has a favourable water depth.

Wells Harbour has been chosen as the operational base for the windfarm, with work in hand to improve tidal access to the harbour and the construction of a new outer jetty with pontoons. Plans are also in hand for the long-term maintenance of the harbour channel to maintain depths at the level required for windfarm vessel access.

Tesco and Toilets

At the time of writing two topics have dominated reports and headlines in the local press. First, the desire of supermarket giant Tesco to achieve their aim of establishing a store in every town in Norfolk, with Sheringham a prime target.

It has been a long, slow fight dating back some 12 years and is an issue which has split the town in two with the pro and anti lobbies becoming quite vociferous and all kinds of red herrings being deployed to back various claims which, at times, have been both entertaining and inaccurate. Following a public inquiry by a government inspector Tesco has been forced to go back to the drawingboard and has engaged a national award-winning firm of architects

to come back with revised proposals for a smaller store than was originally planned.

The whole issue has become complicated by the submission by two other local developers for what they consider to be more logical and/or eco-friendly supermarkets. One, by businessman Richard Davies, proposes putting a store on the town's main car park with both ground-level and underground car parking and the building of 54 'affordable' flats on the site.

The other scheme, by businessman Clive Hay-Smith, has prompted a great deal of interest because his proposal is not just for a supermarket.

In addition to providing additional allotments for existing and future gardeners, a charity-based state-of-the-art cookery and food academy is also planned, where individuals and groups, especially school parties, will be able to 'enhance their skills'. Electrically powered buses will provide a shuttle service around the town, with similarly powered vans providing a doorstep delivery service.

It is anticipated that North Norfolk District Council will make a decision on which application to approve towards the end of 2009. At the end of July 2009 Sainsbury announced they were ready to move into the empty Woolworth's store in the High Street. They intend to open a 2,750sq.ft convenience store and create some 25 jobs.

❖ CHAPTER 8 ❖

Down to the Sea in Ships

Fishing and Fishermen

The earliest evidence of the presence of man in Norfolk, based on primitive tools found, is around 400,000BC, his food for survival coming from hunting and plant gathering. Although fishing is not mentioned, this must have been practised in ponds, lakes, rivers and estuaries. It not being until 7000–6000BC that rising sea levels severed our land connections to what we now know as Europe, at which time our coastline would have been many miles north of where it is today. Again, evidence of primitive fishing practices has come from the finding of a mesolithic fish spear 25 miles north-east of Cromer, and a microlith point found on Kelling Heath. The latter consisted of a worked flint mounted on a rod of either bone, horn or wood, and would have made an ideal spearing fish. We know that fishermen from Upper Sheringham launched their boats from the Old Hythe, about a mile west of

the town of Sheringham, as did fishermen living in the area prior to the compilation of the Domesday Book in 1086.

It was, however, the village of Lower Sheringham which, with its freshwater beck and gentle slope to the beach, soon outgrew Upper Sheringham. As it grew it attracted tradesmen such as rope spinners, sail makers, basket, rope and net makers, twine spinners and net repairers.

Rough wooden buildings were soon replaced with neat flint and pebble-walled cottages. Fish merchants were attracted by the business opportunities and in 1358 they were empowered, provided that other businesses were not 'inconvenienced' and the price of fish did not rise, to buy fish at the already flourishing port of Blakeney. A further help to their businesses arrived in 1374, when local fishermen were exempted from paying a subsidy of 6d. in the pound on catches made

Before the arrival of 'progress' in 1887, with trains

Buying the catch, c.1895. The buyer is wearing a bowler hat and is holding two stones which he will click together in the traditional Sheringham manner to seal the deal. Among the fishermen are possibly 'Downtide' West, 'Cutty' Grice and 'Old Buck' Craske.

Happy to pose for the young photographer are right: *'Bumshie' West, Henry Ward Cooper, Willie Long, Dick Little;* left: *'Tiddley' Middleton, Stanley Little, 'Old Ward' Cooper, 'Old Joe' Little.*

Life was hard for a fisherman's wife. Not only did she run the household, look after the children, cope with her husband's erratic hours and knit his ganseys, she also helped mend his fishing nets and his crab and lobster pots. Seen here are (left) *Mrs Grimes, wife of 'Honey' Grimes and Dorothy Grimes.*

opening a very wide door through which all manner of people could visit this newly discovered seaside resort, fishermen dominated the local political scene simply by force of numbers whenever there was a vote to be taken. Wives of fishermen undoubtedly lived a very hard life. With boys leaving school at 12, or even 10, they were probably called upon to teach their husbands to read and write, were responsible for handling the family money, were expected to have a hot meal ready whatever time he came home from fishing and had to help him prepare bait, mend nets and pots and in general live a life dominated by the fishing industry.

With the arrival of holidaymakers and second homers looking for people to act as baby-minders, nursemaids, cleaners and a host of other duties, fish-

Left to right, back row: 'Old Man' Grice, ?, 'Little Dick' West, 'Sixey' Knowles, James 'Paris' West; front row: James 'Coley' Cooper, three visitors, 'Young George' Grice. (COURTESY MRS M. GAFF)

Sheringham fishermen with their catch of whelks, c.1890.

Sheringham fishermen in the 1800s.

Left to right: *'Brigham' Bishop, Robert West, 'Squinter' West, 'Lotion' Bishop, Robert Cooper, c.1890.*

ermen's wives could suddenly see a vague form of independence opening up, the ultimate decision being to move the family into the outhouse for the summer season and let out their 'quaint' cottage to a visiting family, all meals being provided by the fisherman's wife.

Sheringham crabs and lobsters are caught from selected breeding grounds ½–2½ miles offshore, and whilst the former may be smaller than those caught in other parts of the country, it is claimed they have a better meat content. Plaice are virtually non-existent

due to trawling, whilst salmon, usually caught close inshore, are rare and valuable.

The days of herring fishing are over, although herring can still be caught using drift nets up to 2½ miles offshore.

The 1920s and '30s were the heyday of the whelking industry, Sheringham being described as 'the most important inshore fishing centre on the Norfolk coast, with its 80 boats and 120 fishermen'.

In 1913 the overall income from the fishing trade was said to be £9,000. Harry Johnson, the leading

Edmund, James and Harry Grice preparing whelks at the Whelk Coppers.

Two of the Grice brothers at the Whelk Coppers with Harry Johnson ready to drive to the station.

fishermen in the town at this time, had started his working life as a clerk at the railway station office, where it soon became apparent that he was an astute businessman with the courage of his convictions. He realised the local fishing industry was ripe for redevelopment, with whelking offering great opportunities for expansion.

He soon acquired five coppers and set up business in the cottages which then formed the Whelk Coppers near the lifeboat house on the West Slipway. The coppers themselves, on the western side of the buildings, were operated by local men Ben Smith, Russell Johnson and Joe Farrow. The main boats contracted to Harry Johnson were the *Liberty*, the

123

Left to right: *Gofather Pegg, ?, 'Old Boots' Johnson, Bob 'Hot' Cooper, John Hardingham, Bob Fields, Billy Twell Little, ?, Ernie Grimes, 'Cutty' Lolly Grice, Henry Little* (centre front).

Above: *Cuttlefish caught off Sheringham by Jimmy 'Paris' West. On the Tansley postcard he gives the date as 19 January but doesn't say which year!*

Right: *Gertrude and Tonny 'Dingey' Craske with their daughter Gertrude.*

West End, 1902. Left to right, back row: *Robert 'Old Lolly' Grice, Old Nat Craske, Robert 'Old Butcher' Johnson, Old Barnes Cooper, Old Galton Cooper;* front row: *Christopher 'Old Cutty' Grice, Dick (?) 'Mink' Middleton, Dicky Love, 'Little Dick' West, J. Tailor Love, J. 'Ninny' Craske, Jimmy 'Donny Ha Ha' Hannah, Billy 'Stoner' Hannah, Young Jimmy Mace Johnson.*

Left to right: *Robert Rushmer, 'Sea Toad' Cooper, 'Shrimp' Broome, 'Old Mace' Johnson, Billy Farrow (Beach Inspector).*

Left to right: *Pepper Wilson, Rufus West, George 'Salter' Farrow, Duncan Cooper, John Rook, Robert Willie West, Gofather Pegg, Willie Long (the evangelist), 'Tiddly' Middleton, Henry Cooper.*

By East Beach, near Splash Point. Left to right: *Billy Hannah (Eastern Sea Fisheries officer), 'Old Guinness' Craske, Robert 'Bumshie' West, Henry Ward Cooper.*

The Thalia, *last of the Great Boats.*

Welcome Home, the *Admiral Beatty* and the *White Heather*. Harry bought direct from the fishermen, and sacks of whelks were collected daily by the railway horse and dray, taken to the station and sent within 24 hours to such centres as London, Clacton, Southend and other places, local and nationwide.

Sheringham football team were proud to wear a golden whelk on their shirts and as the town symbol it appeared on locally produced pottery.

The trade flourished up to the outbreak of war in 1939, when the activities at Weybourne anti-aircraft training camp made it difficult and unsafe for fishing to continue in that area. It is understood that the fishermen were compensated for this loss of business.

As part of his fishing industry improvement plans Harry had, in 1914, taken the momentous decision to fit engines in the fishing boats under his control. The practice spread and soon he was exercising his monopoly over the trade as fishermen realised they had to go to him for petrol, servicing and repairs. So profitable did these ventures become that Harry was soon owner of the town's two major hotels, the Grand and the Burlington on the seafront, and had a financial interest in some London properties.

The Great Boats of the mid-1860s resembled the luggers of Great Yarmouth, which fished for herring – the 'silver darlings' of the sea. Because of their size the boats could not be hauled up the town's shingle beach but could be seen either riding at anchor

Fishermen James 'Squinter' West and 'Big' John Craske.

In the 1880s and 1890s Sheringham beaches were busy places, with upwards of 200 boats working from them.

This shark, caught off Sheringham on 24 November 1913, weighed 3cwt and was 7ft long.

offshore or unloading their catches into crab boats to be brought ashore. They were crewed by about a dozen men and carried at least one standard crab boat on deck, this being used during the crabbing season when the pots had to be serviced. If while crabbing off, say, Grimsby they caught any light-brown crabs, known as 'Yorkshiremen', these would be brought back both to sell and to replenish local stocks. The boats would overwinter either at Wells or in Blakeney Pit.

The West family in Sheringham owned three Great Boats, the *New Walter and Ann*, built in Great Yarmouth in 1840, the *Paragon* built at Yarmouth in 1844 and the *Robert and Henry*, built at Cobham in 1877. Of the two boats named *Liberty*, one was owned by a member of the Craske family in Sheringham. The last Great Boat to be owned by a Sheringham fisherman, Philip Wells, was the *Thalia*, built by S.C. Allerton of Lowestoft in 1886. He used it for about six years, after which it was registered in succession at Hull and Lowestoft before being wrecked on a sandbank off the Essex coast in 1918. In October 1880 eight of these boats were caught in a sudden and ferocious storm, during which one of them, the *Gleaner*, from Sheringham and skippered by George 'Coaches' Craske, was overturned and driven ashore at Beeston with the loss of the entire crew of 11 local men,

James West and his son, also James, were typical of the many Sheringham fishermen who, in the late 1870s and '80s were so affected by falling fish prices that they decided to seek a better life elsewhere. They simply packed what worldly goods they possessed into their fishing boat and set sail for Grimsby, where they hoped to find a new and better life with more productive fishing and improved markets. Once there they made their way to that part of their new homeland already known as 'Shannockland' or 'Little Sheringham' in an area incorporating such streets as Charles Street, Victor Street, Hope Street and Castle Street, where the Norfolk accent and dialect were already known. In the early days, as they established themselves, times were hard, with sparrow pie a frequent item on the daily menu. The Sheringham immigrants were devoutly religious and most were members of the Salvation Army. As in Sheringham, they formed a 'Songster Brigade' and toured their new home singing at Army meetings and other venues.

Within a very short space of time most of the Grimsby lifeboat crew were 'Shannockers', as was the congregation of the Salvation Army citadel, built with the help of several ex-Sheringham fishermen, some of whom carved the pulpit.

Fishermen have always been superstitious individuals with hard-held beliefs that very simple actions or occurrences could affect their livelihoods.

If, for instance, a clergyman was seen before launching, the fishing trip could well be cancelled.

'Old' Billy Butcher Johnson (father) and 'Young' Billy Butcher Johnson (son).

Left to right: *Billy 'Click' Bishop, 'Shrimp' Broom, Charles Holsey.*

There would be no fishing on a Friday, women were not allowed in the boat and certainly were never taken on a fishing trip. A piece of coal had to be put into the boat before launching and it was strictly forbidden to mention any animal before going to sea.

Old Fiddy West.

Rufus and Martha West.

It has always been the custom among fishing families to give sons the same Christian name as their fathers. This would have caused, and still does cause, some confusion. Had you been in Sheringham some years ago looking for a Mr Henry Grice without knowing that there were about a dozen fishermen answering to the name! If, however, you had known his nickname, the problem was instantly solved.

Nicknames are often based on some personal habit or physical feature, as in 'Squinter' West, 'Bounce' Craske (because of a definite bounce in the way he walked), or on some quirk of personality by which he is remembered by his colleagues, as in 'Spitfire' Farrow, because of his quick reactions to any problem or occurrence. Had the author of this book been born into a fishing family he could be rejoicing in the nickname 'Scribbler', or 'Wordy'.

The Other Occupation

If fishing was the main industry in both Upper and Lower Sheringham, then the second most important source of employment was agriculture, with some ten farms being recorded either within or on the town's boundaries. Manor Farm House was situated on what is now the Morris Street car park, and

during research for another local history book a few years ago the author was told by elderly Shannocks that it was within living memory that cattle had been driven through the streets of Sheringham on their way to market.

It was remembered, too, that during autumn and winter months, when bad weather made fishing impossible, some fishermen sought work on the land. Certainly, for the sons of fishermen, skiving off from school was a regular occurrence at harvest time. Other jobs open to young-lads included crow scaring for 1s.6d. a day, leading horses at seed-drilling time, manure spreading and beating during the pheasant season. It was not unusual for boys to work a 12-hour day, or even longer, for the princely sum of 6d.

Stanley Craske recorded an average day for a boy labourer, who would start at 6a.m. and work through to 11a.m., give the horses a break and food, then work through to 6.30–7p.m. Winter months would include such work as pulling up and cleaning swedes and turnips, herding sheep and feeding cattle, all for a 'wage' of 3s. for a six-day week. The full-time farm labourer lived a hard life. Many of them worked a six or seven day week, including spells at Christmas and other Bank Holidays, all for a wage of around 11s. a week to a retirement age of between 75 and 80. Harvest suppers were, by all accounts, the highlights of the farming year. In a wagon decorated with flowers, children, dressed up, would ride round the village together with farm labourers, dressed as scarecrows or country bumpkins, busy with their collecting tins. The money they collected, together with a donation from the farmer, helped pay for the supper to be held in a cleaned and decorated barn. The tables would be laden with beef, pork, game and other delicacies rarely seen in the workers' cottages. In addition, there would be beer for the men, soft drinks for the children and tea for wives and sweethearts. After the meal there could be dancing to a fiddler's music, but not until too late, as it would be back to work in the morning!

The Rioting Fishermen

On 12 January 1874 nine Sheringham fishermen appeared in court at the Tollhouse, Great Yarmouth, facing the charge that on the night of 10 November 1874 they had banded together 'for the purpose of riot with cries and ejaculations showing plainly they had confederated together for a certain purpose'. It was further alleged that whilst there might have been some 'little quarrel' between one or two Yarmouth and Sheringham men, this 'would form no excuse for the conduct of the Sheringham men in knocking down and injuring peaceable townsfolk'. Both policemen and townspeople testified they saw 'a number of men coming out of the Odd Fellows Tavern and the Foundry Arms at about ten minutes past 11 crying out: 'Stick together Sheringham men', a phrase repeated as they walked along, sometimes with the additional words: 'Let's give it to the Yarmouth *****!. It was further alleged that the nine men approached pedestrians asking them if they were Yarmouth people. If the answer was 'Yes', they were 'knocked down'. Some of the men allegedly threw stones at policemen.

At the bottom of Friars Lane a little boy named Wales was knocked down and kicked 'by three or four men'. It was said that no Yarmouth people were involved in the disturbances. Two were 'very much frightened and went to the police for protection'.

One witness said he saw more then 150 men come out of the two inns but did not hear the word 'Shannock' used. The Recorder, Mr Sims Reeve, asked for the meaning of the word, but no one present in court knew. It was thought not to be complimentary, but Mr Sims Reeve thought it was a very nice word (there was laughter in court!).

It was alleged that the Sheringham fishermen 'knocked over' 20–30 people, five or six of them attacking a single person before knocking him, or her, to the ground and then kicking them.

One of the witnesses had followed the Sheringham men back to the wharf and said that they seemed mad 'and were in drink although they were not absolutely drunk'. One of the fishermen, on hearing one of the Yarmouth policemen blowing his whistle, allegedly cried out: 'You may blow your whistle, you *****! We'll kill all you ***** Yarmouth police tonight.'

It was said there were five or six boats belonging to the Sheringham men lying at the Fish Wharf, the biggest of these being the Great Boat *Welcome Home*, owned by Joshua Henry West and others and skippered by John Long. One of the Sheringham men was accused of 'jumping about and saying he would kill people'. Several witnesses said they had been 'knocked down' by the Sheringham men, one to the point of insensibility. For the defence it was stated that the Sheringham fishermen had to defend themselves against the Yarmouth men and that one of them had been an abstainer for ten months. All the defendants, it was stated, had good characters and there had been no riot. It was 'a common row', and if there was any class of men in England deserving sympathy it was the fishermen. Against this the

Section of an early painting by an unknown artist showing the fishing boat Upcher *saving the crew of the* Elizabeth, *1828.* (COURTESY ROBIN AND LINDA WEST)

An early etching of the Upcher *rescuing the crew of a ship off Sheringham. It was her role as an unofficial lifeboat that led to the provision of a formal service to protect the local fishing fleet.*

The Augusta *lifeboat and crew.* In the boat, left to right: *'Old John Tar' Bishop, 'Old Rook' Reynolds, 'Old Skye' Johnson, 'Old John' Craske, Kiffer Johnson, John Farrow, 'Dogless' Farrow, John Long, 'Spider' Johnson, 'Tipoo' Cooper, 'Uncle' Johnson, 'Maggot' Johnson, Dick 'Twirl' Little, Billy Johnson, 'Cockney' Cox, 'Butcher' Johnson, 'Crib' Craske, Barnes Cooper, 'Squinter West';* standing by the boat: *'Dingey' Craske, 'Ta Ra Ra Boomdeeay' Grice, 'Butter Balls' Grice, 'Ready' Johnson, Billy Johnson, 'Belcher' Johnson, 'Saffron' Grimes, 'Jockey' Grimes, 'King Kong' Grice, 'Lolly' Grice, 'Salter' Farrow.*

A rare picture of the Augusta *and crew.*

prosecution said that six of the defendants had been previously involved in a riot at a Cromer carnival, and one had been convicted for being drunk and riotous. When it came to judgement three of the fishermen, John Long, Alfred Love and Matthew Scotter, were found not guilty. Edward Craske and Charles West were each sentenced to prison for two months, and Edmund Grice, Henry Middleton and Robert Middleton were fined £5 each or, in default, prison for one month.

In returning their verdicts the jury said they were satisfied that James Grice had a knife in his hand and that Craske and West were the ringleaders of the rest. James Grice was sent to prison for three months with hard labour.

In a surprising afternote to the trial, it was 'understood' that the fishermen who had been fined and were perhaps unable to pay had been 'bailed out' by the Upcher family of Sheringham Hall.

The Sea Shall Not Have Them

With over 170 years of lifeboat history Sheringham can rightly claim to be proud of its lifesaving role along a part of the North Norfolk coastline known as the 'Devil's Throat'.

The first recorded rescue carried out by a local boat off this part of the Norfolk coast has never been dated, but it must have been after 1812, when Abbott Upcher bought the Sheringham estate. Confirmation of this comes in the form of a primitive painting of a local fishing boat with the name *Upcher* rescuing the crew of a sailing ship, c.1820.

The year 1836 was not a good one for Sheringham. It is remembered for its storms and the loss of seven fishermen from the Little, Craske, Wilson and Bishop families. So moved was Caroline Upcher, widowed following the death of her husband, Abbott, that she commissioned Robert Sunman, wheelwright and boat builder of Upper Sheringham, to build the first designated lifeboat to serve Sheringham. It was to be built in the grounds of Sheringham Hall using local oak to a design resembling the existing fishing boats but bigger, with a length of 33ft 6 ins, a breadth of 10ft 2ins, a depth of 4ft 2ins and with 16 oars. The cost was £150 and she was launched on 14 November 1838. She was named *Augusta* in memory of Abbott's and Caroline's youngest daughter, who had died from tuberculosis at the tragically early age of 20.

During the next few years the lifeboat saved some 51 lives, the largest group being from a Russian barque. Many local lives were also saved, endangered fishermen being taken out of their boats and brought to safety. In the case of the Russian ship the

On the morning of Saturday, 26 November 1988 Sheringham traffic was brought to a standstill by 300 people who met at the town clock to celebrate the 150th anniversary of lifeboat service in the town. During the year more than 50 events were organised to celebrate the voluntary service of men always ready to risk their lives in order to save others.

Henry Ramey Upcher, *'the fishermen's lifeboat'*, 1894–1935, can still be seen in her original boathouse on the West Slipway.

captain, whilst agreeing that his crew could leave the vessel, insisted he leave a cabin boy aboard. When he was told it was 'all or none' he raised the sails and began to make his way up the coast with the *Augusta* following. The lifeboatmen pointed out the danger facing the captain and crew but the reply came back that they were perfectly safe and knew where they were, whereupon the captain pointed to Blakeney church and named it as Dover Castle! When corrected he and all of his crew 'tumbled over one another' into the lifeboat and were rescued. Emma Pigott later recorded: 'A piece of hard black bread from the Russian ship lay on my mother's library table for years afterwards.' The *Augusta* served Sheringham faithfully for over 50 years before she developed 'nail sickness', rendering her unsuitable to

Launching the Henry Ramey Upcher *on Saturday, 11 May 1935 to go to the aid of local fishing boats.*

The Henry Ramey Upcher *in full sail. Her usual crew consisted of coxswain, deputy coxswain, 16 oars, eight men to organise the sails and two men on pumps, a total of 24 men.*

face the rigours of battling the wild North Sea. Unfortunately, few records were kept of her rescues, so the true number of lives she saved is unknown, though reliable sources have suggested that 1,000 could be a reliable estimate.

In the late 1940s she was donated to the Norfolk Boy Scouts to use on The Broads and when, in 1951, she was considered to be irreparable she was sawn in half and used as two sheltered garden seats.

In 1988 the 150th anniversary year of lifeboats in Sheringham, there were many celebrations, culminating in November when upwards of 300 people, mostly wearing *Augusta* commemorative t-shirts, gathered in the town centre for a celebrity photograph. I did ask the publishers of this book if they would like all the people in the photograph to be named, but they politely declined my invitation!

One of Sheringham's claims to fame, which has never been challenged, is that it is the only place in the world to possess four of its original lifeboats. The oldest of these is the *Henry Ramey Upcher*, which can be seen in her original lifeboat shed at the top of the West Slipway.

Like her predecessor, she was donated to the town by a member of the Upcher family, this time by Mrs Caroline Upcher, who named the boat in memory of her late husband. The boat was built by another local man, Lewis Emery, of Lower Sheringham in his two-storey workshop on Lifeboat Plain. He worked, like most boatbuilders of his generation, 'by eye and thumb', using skills learned from his father and his own experience. Emery boats were always in great demand, and working fishing boats can still be found along the east coast from Grimsby to Great Yarmouth. Uniquely, they never underwent a preliminary sea trial before being handed over to the customer. They were usually collected by the new owner and went straight into service, and the author knows of no case where any fault in the construction of a boat was found.

The *Henry Ramey* was launched on 4 September

The lifeboat Duncan, *her crew all wearing cork lifejackets.* (COURTESY M. PAYNE)

1894 and named by Caroline Upcher. During her life-time she was launched well in excess of 50 times and has been credited with saving over 200 lives.

In their book *The Story of the Sheringham Lifeboats*, Linda and Robin West cite an entry from the lifeboat's log in 1913 in which a stranded fisherman from Sea Palling had heard of the *Ramey's* reputation for rescuing not only fishermen but also their nets and associated gear. He and his companion tried to head toward Sheringham and were met by the *Ramey* who took them in tow, beached them safely and then sold their catch of mackerel for them. As the Palling fisherman said, he would always remember the kindness of the lifeboat crew, without whose help he would have lost his boat and nets and been at least £50 out of pocket.

Among the lifeboats rescues were 14 men from the 546-ton steamer *Commodore*, driven ashore just west of Sheringham during a gale. Within a few days the ship was a wreck, with debris scattered along the beach. Soon only a sizeable piece of the bow was left, and this remained on the beach for nearly seven years until Trinity House finally ordered it to be blown up. On Saturday, 23 January 1897 the Norwegian brig *Ispolen* was driven ashore at Sheringham, the sea so rough that when the *Ramey* approached her the lifeboat was swept onto the deck of the brig, suffering some damage. On a second attempt the crew of the lifeboat managed to throw and fix some grappling hooks to the brig's super-structure, enabling the eight-man crew to jump into the lifeboat, which took them to the Two Lifeboats Hotel, where they were given hot food and dry clothes. Given the right weather, a north-easterly wind and a scouring tide, parts of the keel of the *Ispolen* can still be seen on the West Beach.

In April 1866 the RNLI sent their Inspector of Lifeboats to Norfolk to determine the most suitable location for one of their boats. After a full coastal survey he chose Sheringham, the actual site being on the East Cliff. Mr Henry Upcher provided land for the building of a new Lifeboat House, and a donation from Mrs Agnes Fraser (née Duncan) in memory of her father and an uncle paid the cost of a new lifeboat, fittingly named the *Duncan*.

The new lifeboat and her carriage were brought by rail to Fakenham, the Great Eastern Railway waiving all costs as their contribution to the lifeboat service. The journey to Sheringham was completed by road on a carriage drawn by horses lent by Mr Hardy and Mr Upcher.

When discussions started on the type of lifeboat house to be provided, the local vicar, Revd Lethbridge Moore, expressed the wish to make this occasion one 'morally and spiritually profitable to the fishing portion of the inhabitants of the parish'. He proposed that the new building should not just be a lifeboat house, and the opportunity was taken to incorporate a reading and lecture room for the use of fishermen. The national committee of the RNLI agreed to this and to meet two-thirds of the total cost, the vicar undertaking to meet the remainder. Three estimates were received from local men, that in the sum of £251 (£151 for the boathouse and £100 for the reading and lecture room) from Mr Francis being accepted. Two sites for the new building were considered, that 'opposite the coalyard and the coal-yard gangway' on land we now know as Lifeboat Plain being agreed, the RNLI being responsible for keeping the gangway in 'practical repair'. We now know the Lifeboat House as the Oddfellows Hall, named after the Friendly Society of the same name, who bought the building in 1931. Now thoroughly restored and renovated, seen from the top of Gun Street it presents a striking appearance.

The day of 4 October 1883 was an unusual one for many people. The brigantine *Alpha*, bound from Faversham to Whitstable with a full load of coal, was seen flying a signal of distress. As she was nearer to Cromer than Sheringham, the coxswain of the latter lifeboat did not go to her assistance, a decision for which he was reprimanded 'for his error of judgement'. The vessel grounded on Cromer beach and swiftly became a wreck, with the five-man crew seen clinging to the bowsprit. 'To the surprise of all' Cromer lifeboat did not go to her assistance and the local rocket brigade failed to make contact. With time

A rare photograph of the J.C. Madge *in sail. The last of the town's pulling and sailing lifeboats, she served from 1904 to 1936.*

slipping by, the threat to the crew was becoming increasingly dangerous and a message was sent to Sheringham for aid. In order to save time it was decided that the *Duncan* should be sent to Cromer by road. On the way the carriages and horses stopped off at Runton in an effort to launch her, but without success. By this time the *Alpha* had split in two and of the Sheringham fishermen who had arrived on the scene some waded through the surf to rescue the crew of the ship. Edward Craske and Robert Bishop saved four of the five men, the last being brought ashore by a Cromer Coastguard. They were helped in the rescues by 11 other unnamed Sheringham fishermen. During her 19 years of service the *Duncan* is credited with saving 18 lives. Because of difficulties in negotiating the slipway she frequently worked in cooperation with the private lifeboat *Augusta*, which was lighter and often reached vessels in distress before the *Duncan*.

On 20 July 1885 a meeting of fishermen, although they thought highly of the *Duncan*, made it clear they wanted a new lifeboat, simpler, lighter and better adapted to local conditions. It should also, they agreed, have a longer keel, be greater in beam, carry a larger spread of canvas and pull more than 12 oars. It was further stipulated that the new boat should be supplied complete with an anchor and a hauling rope and the oars should be made of deal. It was also decided that Robert Davidson should be appointed as permanent coxswain and that William Craske should be his assistant.

Henry Johnson, Harry Grice and Robert Grice were invited to visit the RNLI's head office to 'look over' new lifeboats and make their choice of which one they thought best for Sheringham. They chose the *William Bennett*, 40ft long, 9ft 3ins in beam and 'combining all the latest improvements'. It left

Launching the lifeboat J.C. Madge *on her original carriage from the Old Hythe Lifeboat House.*

(COURTESY SHERINGHAM MUSEUM)

London on 6 July 1886 by sea, its carriage coming by rail to Cromer. It arrived in Sheringham the following day, although the carriage did not.

This news was not received with pleasure by the chairman of the RNLI, Colonel Fitzroy Clayton, for whom a demonstration had been organised. His displeasure increased when the winch used to pull the lifeboat up the sand and shingle beach broke down. For the fishermen, and lifeboatmen too, there was disappointment when it was discovered that far from being lighter than her predecessor, the new lifeboat was, in fact, a good deal heavier and posed serious difficulties when moving through a narrow access point to a difficult gangway. So serious did these difficulties become that for the last four years of intended service the lifeboat was parked in Beach Road covered with a tarpaulin. By 1903 parts of the boat were found to be rotten and a deputation of Sheringham lifeboatmen visited the lifeboat station along the East Coast to identify which type of lifeboat was best suited for Sheringham. The men came back with a recommendation that Sheringham should have '... a boat of the Liverpool type', of larger dimensions, if possible, than the boat at Cromer. The RNLI's response was to send the 41ft clinker-built *J.C. Madge*, the largest of the Liverpool-type lifeboats and the second of Sheringham's preserved historic lifeboats. Indeed, so highly is she valued that this lifeboat is included in the National Register of Historic Vessels in the United Kingdom. She takes her name from a Mr Madge, who was a chemist in Southampton and a generous supporter of the RNLI. She sailed from Blackwall on 30 November 1904, stopping twice on her way here, arriving in Sheringham on 2 December. Awaiting her was a new lifeboat house, a corrugated-iron building erected in 1942 at the Old Hythe, a dip in the cliffs about a mile west of Sheringham. She was officially named at a ceremony on the site on 13 December 1904.

When the crew were called out the quickest way to get from the town to the lifeboat house was to run across the golf course, the first 16 men to arrive claiming a full set of protective clothing, including the all-important cork lifejacket.

Jimmy 'Paris' West told the author he was a very fit young crew member in those days, but he was often outrun by other crew members well into their 60s and 70s. He also said that once you had learned the technique it was possible to jump from the cliff onto the curved corrugated iron roof and slide down to land on the soft sand near the boathouse entrance!

When I asked if he could swim I was met with a scornful look and a reply I shall never forget: 'We wore high boots with leaded soles and heels. If the Good Lord wanted you it was best to go straight down without any struggling.' This philosophy was shared by many of his colleagues and underlined their deep religious beliefs.

Within a very short time of starting life in her new home it was realised that the soft sand made launching and beaching difficult, slowing down rescue times and demanding a great deal of human effort before the crew faced the intimidating waves of the North Sea. There is no doubt which of the *Madge*'s call outs was the most harrowing in terms of those awaiting her safe return. On 24 February 1914 the SS *Uller* of Bergen became grounded on the Dudgeon Sands before floating off damaged and leaking. She then want aground again, this time off Blakeney, before floating off into deep water. With the Cromer and Wells lifeboats unable to launch because of the atrocious weather the *Madge* launched with great difficulty, the crew being drenched by the first wave they met, which threatened to completely bury the *Madge* and every member of her crew.

On reaching the *Uller* they found the captain desperately trying to keep her afloat, so they stood by her in terrible conditions all night. Come morning the captain decided to make for Grimsby, the *Madge* being towed behind and in very real danger of being

The lifeboat Foresters Centenary.

During the Second World War troops were often called on to help launch and land the lifeboat.

thrown against the big ship's propeller. On arrival at Grimsby the *Uller* was redirected to Hull. The crew of the *Madge* stayed overnight in Grimsby safe in the knowledge that a government ship in the port had promised to send a message back to Sheringham saying the lifeboat crew were safe and well. Unfortunately no such message was sent.

In Sheringham, the lifeboat having been absent for four days, all hope of seeing her again was gone, and local churchmen were already starting to call on families of the crew offering spiritual guidance and condolences. Funeral services were also being planned. Think, then, of the unimaginable joy when her familiar shape was seen from the beach as she came over the horizon, and the happiness of reunion with wives, sweethearts, sons, daughters and other relatives of men thought lost to the greedy sea. The year 1936 was quite a momentous one for the lifeboat service in Sheringham. A new lifeboat house was nearing completion at the end of the west promenade and our first motorised lifeboat, the *Foresters Centenary*, arrived to begin her 25 years of service, which included the fateful years of the Second World War, during which she earned her second name, 'the airmen's lifeboat', because of the number of airmen saved from a watery grave in the North Sea. Built by Groves & Gutteridge on the Isle of Wight, she had been donated to the RNLI by the Ancient Order of Foresters Friendly Society to commemorate the society's centenary. Whilst awaiting the completion of the new lifeboat house the lifeboat was kept at the Old Hythe, where she was named on 18 July 1936 by Admiral of the Fleet Sir Roger Keyes. Without a

turntable or a carriage, launching and beaching of the lifeboat had to be done manually, it not always being appreciated just how many men were needed to carry out these simple sounding tasks; any number under 50 and you could be in difficulties; any number over, preferably approaching 100, and you could manage. During the war years many soldiers found themselves being directed to decidedly unsoldierly tasks with the distinct possibility of getting their feet wet!

During her time at Sheringham the *Foresters* is credited with saving 91 men, 16 of them airmen, and recovered the bodies of three aircrew. Although wartime rescues always have an element of excitement, there is one incident that remains unsolved.

During the night of 29 January 1940 mechanic Teddy Craske picked up a message on his short-wave radio which simply said 'East Dudgeon Lightship being bombed by a German plane'. The lifeboat was immediately launched, but on reaching the lightship its lifeboat was missing and the light was broken, as were the wheelhouse windows; there was no sign of life. The *Foresters* crew assumed the lighthouse crew had either been picked up by a passing ship or had followed the tide down towards Great Yarmouth. A long search east of the lightship proved abortive, and the lifeboat returned home.

The lightship crew, in fact, had turned west, where their boat was driven ashore by a heavy sea with the tragic loss of all but one of them.

The mystery of this incident? Simply that the lightship did not have a radio; so where did the message that it was being bombed come from? The only explanation would appear to be that a crew member of the attacking aircraft had a conscience.

On 9 February 1940 the *Foresters* went to the aid of the *Boston Trader*, on fire after being attacked by a German aircraft. The Coastguard had reported seeing a small boat leave the ship, and by the time our lifeboat arrived on the scene just a few inches of the boat remained above sea level. Without the prompt arrival of the lifeboat the ship's crew would have drowned.

On 21 October 1940 the Coastguard reported a plane in the sea off Blakeney. It was early morning, dark and raining, but a member of the *Foresters* thought he saw a light. It turned out to be from a rubber dinghy holding five bomber crew who, returning from a raid on a German target, were forced to ditch in the North Sea.

Five days later a Wellington bomber returning from a raid on Hamburg also had to ditch in the sea on its way back home. Five members of its Polish crew managed to get out only to spend a cold and foggy night and the next day drifted eastwards along the North Norfolk coast. They were lost and disoriented but luck was with them. The landlord of the Crown Inn just happened to be looking out to sea and thought he saw a speck on the horizon. Using a tele-

The lifeboat Manchester Unity of Oddfellows.

scope he could see figures on what he thought was a raft. The lifeboat was launched. They found five very tired and hungry Polish airmen who were soon landed and given a remedial mixture of rum, chocolate and biscuits. Because of their growing friendship with crews from East Anglia-based aerodromes the crew of the *Foresters* were invited to visit them and so their nickname – the 'airmen's lifeboat' – was born. A relationship was strengthened at the time of the 1,000 bomber raids, when the sky over Sheringham was filled with heavy bombers ordered into formation by specially decorated control planes. As one resident recorded: 'The ground literally vibrated with the noise from so many powerful engines.' This was the period during which the lifeboat had to spend the night well out to sea ready to go to the aid of any aircraft forced to ditch following damage from anti-aircraft fire or attack from enemy fighters.

The *Foresters Centenary* came out of service on 2 June 1961 and was sent to Oulton Broad to be sold. Some time later the Museum Trust discovered she was working on the Blackwater Estuary as a hire boat available to fishermen and fishing parties, and that her owner was looking to change her for a new craft. Negotiations to buy her were successful and she was brought back to Sheringham, where a team of volunteer fishermen, lifeboatmen, sailors and boat owners dedicated years of their lives to restoring this historic lifeboat to its original condition. They may not have been technically qualified, but, more importantly, they knew boats and had lived with them for many years. The previous owners of the lifeboat, John and Garry Shaw, visited Sheringham during the restoration work and Garry spent some holiday time working with our volunteers. He and his father, John, also provided practical help by collecting the engine from Chatham and bringing it to Sheringham. The cuddy was donated by another friend, Frank Muirhead from Cromer, who had used it as a shed in his garden.

Our first traditional offshore lifeboat, the *Manchester Unity of Oddfellows*, arrived in Sheringham on 10 July 1961 and remained here until 1990, during which time she is credited with saving 94 lives, 65 of these being participants in the 1988 raft race during the August carnival week, when a sudden change in weather conditions brought the race to a sudden and unexpected end, a decision made all the more urgent because some of the participants were not wearing lifejackets. She was originally fitted with twin 43hp Perkins diesel engines, these being replaced by twin 52hp engines in 1986 during a £50,000 refit.

Her service record lists are, as with all the lifeboats, a masterpiece of laconic understatement. Phrases such as 'escorted (fishing) boats' and 'gave help' belie the relief and assurance the lifeboat's presence must have given fishermen and others as they sought their living from an unforgiving sea.

The *Manchester Unity* was to be the last traditional lifeboat to serve Sheringham, for in 1992 the RNLI decided to downgrade the town's lifeboat status to inshore lifeboats only, a decision which seemed perverse to many people, especially to fishermen and lifeboatmen, bearing in mind the town's proud history of lifeboat service.

We were, however, not to lose our relationship with the Manchester Unity of Oddfellows Friendly Society. When the television programme 'Blue Peter' launched its annual appeal for another Blue Peter lifeboat in November 1993 the society subscribed the cost of a new three-man Atlantic inshore lifeboat, named by its Grand Master, Mr. J.W. Goulding at a ceremony on 7 August 1994. Not only this, but the society bought the offshore boat back from the RNLI and presented it to the town for care and restoration ready for display in the new museum. We have now progressed from Atlantic 21 class lifeboats to Atlantic 85 class boats, it being generally agreed that they have proved their worth with greater manoeuvrability, a smoother ride for the three to four-man crew and a speed that enables them to reach a vessel in distress quicker than more traditional lifeboats.

Whilst a lifeboat is always a very visible sign of something happening, this is not true of those people behind the scenes who are responsible for the smooth running of its support services. For the record, therefore, I feel it only right to pay tribute to those volunteers without whom we would not have the efficient lifeboat service we see today.

Sheringham RNLI Branch Committee, 2009
Paul Hawes – Chairman
John Barnett – Treasurer
Mick Halford – Deputy Treasurer
Dr Peter Sampson – Honorary Medical Adviser
Mary Blyth – Souvenir Secretary, Boathouse
Ann Little – Souvenir Secretary, High Street Shop
Bob Parish – Stock Controller, Lifeboat Station
Rita Smith – in charge of box collection
David Mann
Clive Payment
Trevor Holsey
Billie Thirtle

Sheringham Through the Years

Frederick Lincoln was an early trader in Sheringham, specialising in fruits and New Zealand lamb.

James Ardley bought Lincoln's business in 1910. He prided himself on his home delivery service, whereby any item, however small, would instantly be delivered to any part of town.

Sheringham Through the Years

Beeston Common in the early 1900s.

Warby's Mill, just off the A148 Cromer to Holt road, in the early 1900s.

Sheringham Through the Years

The shop of James Henry Pratt, c.1913. According to visitors the only thing that changed over the years was the thickness of the dust on the shelves!

Henry Page's shop in the High Street, c.1915. The company started trading in Aylsham, moving to Sheringham in the early 1900s. It was soon established as one of the top grocers in the county. In those days a member of staff would call to collect your order and arrange for it to be delivered the same week.

Sheringham Through the Years

Colling's & Wilkins, Station Road, in 2009 Jacqueline's shoe shop. Left to right: Charles Collings, Mrs Rose Collings, Miss Wilkins.

Walter Starling's grocer's shop, Wyndham Street, c.1908. He was previously in partnership with Charles William Clarke, who is standing in the doorway, later leaving to establish his own grocery business in Beeston Road. Walter went on to specialise in confectionery, stationery and allied items.

R.C. West was situated on the corner of Church Street and Waterbank Road. The premises were later taken over by coal merchants Bessey & Palmer.

Sheringham Through the Years

Delivering milk to the tea room, in 2009 the Jolly Tar, in Station Road,

Beales's supply stores and Beeston Regis Post Office, January 1934. (COURTESY R.M. HEDGES)

C.W. Clarke, Beeston Road, c.1921. Mr and Mrs Clarke are standing in the doorway.

Smith & Co. florist's shop, Station Road. In 2009 it is a charity shop.

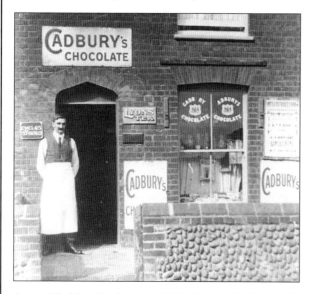

James Gladden Craske outside his shop in Station Road. In 1924 it was sold to Bob Durrant, who ran it as a general grocery store. In the early 1930s he moved to new premises across the road and his former premises were taken over by Mr Hunt, who converted it to a radio shop.

Sid Hastings outside his fruiterer's shop in Augusta Street, c.1960.

Sheringham Through the Years

A knife-grinder's cart, Augusta Street

Sheringham Fire Brigade at the corner of Augusta Street with Church Street. At the scene are Albert Storey (standing on engine), *'Garibaldi' Crowe* (centre, looking at camera), *Walter 'Crook' Sadler* (centre of group on right), *'Blakeney' Bob Warman* (far right), *Mr Hedley* (bald-headed man behind pipe).

Sheringham Through the Years

Victoria Street, early 1900s.

The Marble Arch, built in 1905. Note the stained-glass windows in the toilets.

Sheringham Through the Years

Beeston Road, early 1900s.

Church Street, August 1935. Jarrold's is on the right, with Major Dunn's Central Garage to the left of the Town Clock. Bradley's clothes store is next to Barclay's Bank, with Arthur's butcher's to the left of the bank.

(COURTESY R.M. HEDGES)

147

Sheringham Through the Years

The Police Station (left), *St Peter's Road, 1935. It is now a private house, although the original police cell survives. R.A. Blackwell and Barrett's House Agency were further down the road.*

The bottom of Beach Road, 1933. 'The Mo' (building on right) *was used to train troops in the art of house-to-house fighting. 'The Hazard'* (top left) *is now a car park.*

Sheringham Through the Years

C.W. Dennis's butcher's shop, Cooperative Street. Left to right: John Childs, Charles Dennis, Renee (Charles's *daughter), Stanley Childs, Charlie Long. When C.W. Dennis retired in 1960 the business was taken over by Stanley Childs. It was sold again in 1972 to Mr Andrew Krankis, who installed a manager, Mr Jonas. Miss Joan Thirtle was receptionist and cashier at the shop for over 30 years. The premises were later converted back to a private dwelling.*

The High Street entrance to Central Garage, 1934. Note the old hand-turned petrol pump. Michael Mann can remember that when petrol overflowed when filling a tank it would run down the pavement gutter. The old petrol storage tank is still under the pavement near the Clock Tower.

Charlotte Upcher as a young woman.

Abbot Upcher.

The Honorable Charlotte Upcher.

Henry Ramey Upcher, Charlotte's son.

CHAPTER 9

The Upcher Connection

When Peter Upcher, a gentleman farmer living in Ormesby, died, his only surviving son, Abbot, inherited his estate and became a young man of considerable worth.

In 1808 he attended a public breakfast and dance in Great Yarmouth, where he met his future wife, Charlotte Wilson, the 18-year-old daughter of the Revd Henry Wilson of Kirby Cane. Their first son, Henry Ramey, was born on 8 March 1810, followed by a daughter, Charlotte Mary, in 1811. Abbot, with a growing family to support (they eventually had three sons and three daughters) and living for brief periods at Thomson, near Watton, and then at Great Yarmouth, started to look around for a new and permanent home. After turning down properties at Wroxham and Bagthorpe he chose the Sheringham estate owned by Mr Cook Flower, finding great pleasure in 'the beautiful and romantic grounds but disappointment in the house'. On Wednesday, 10 July 1811, Abbot signed the agreement for the purchase of the estate, the price of £52,500 guineas being partly funded by the sale of his 'scattered' farms in Suffolk and Essex. He was represented in the negotiations by William Repton of Aylsham, whose father was renowned landscape gardener Henry Repton, whom Abbot engaged to design a new mansion. Repton later described Sheringham Bower as his 'favourite and darling child' in Norfolk. His Red Book, containing details of his designs, is still in private ownership.

On 13 October 1812 Abbot and his family came to take possession of their new home, although they had to wait three more days before they could enjoy their first meal there. An early suggestion of naming the new hall 'Marina' was not pursued, and it became known as 'Sheringham Bower'. An entry in Abbot's diary for 12 January 1813 tells us he was developing 'very great pleasure' from farming, and was digging holes for 500 spruce firs on Bunkers Hill.

On the same day there is a reference which sums up Abbot's Christian and charitable attitude to his tenants: 'Yellow-wash'd (stone colour) all the cottages belonging to me and got them glazed and made comfortable, being much out of repair.'

The year 1813 proved to be a busy one for Abbot. He took the opportunity, as churchwarden, to have all the side windows in Upper Sheringham Church made to open and for the church to be whitewashed. The pulpit was moved to the right-hand side of the church and the chancel was painted. In one of his other roles, as surveyor to the parish, he had the old parish house – '... an eyesore and disgrace to Sheringham' – demolished so that the church '... now boldly opens to the street and our woods are made visible to the traveller'.

As you read through the family diaries it becomes increasingly clear that Sheringham had truly been blessed with a new squire. On Christmas Eve 1813 Abbot and Charlotte '... gave away four sheep and four stone of beef to the poor of Sheringham – 72 families; 334lbs of meat for their Xmas dinner.' On Christmas Day they recorded that between 80 and 100 'poor people' received the Sacrament at Sheringham Church. Afterwards: 'All our servants, wives and families dined in our kitchen and the children danced in the nursery with Esther and nurses and Bell played to them on his fiddle.'

Abbot also expressed 'great happiness' that he had managed to reconcile the domestic feuds and quarrels of two families and persuaded the son of the principal farmer in the parish to marry his mistress.

January 1814 saw the arrival of some of the harshest weather for several years, with roads to Holt, Cromer and Aylsham completely blocked by snow. As a result Abbot and Charlotte gave nearly half a ton of coal to the poor of Sheringham. Charlotte was also busy establishing a new women's organisation, the Female Friendly Society, and had recruited 79 members by the end of the year. Abbot was 'happy' to donate five guineas in support. The Society closed in 1857, the year Charlotte died.

Not all of Repton's recommendations were brought to completion, the building of a temple being one, although, so determined was he that such an ornamental building should be built that he wrote a short playlet that began:

The Gods from Olympus have met to debate on the news that had come up from Norfolk of late. How a Temple at Sheringham planned by one Repton was proposed to be raised and inscribed to Neptune because it commanded a view of the sea.

Abbot's untimely death, however, put all thoughts of building a temple to one side, and it was not until Saturday, 17 July 1976 that Thomas Upcher, great-great-grandson of Abbot, was able to call on the Duke of Bedford metaphorically to unveil the temple we now see. Why the Duke of Bedford? Simply because the Duke's grandmother, known as 'the Flying Duchess', once flew over Sheringham Hall and liked the look of the house and estate so much

The Temple at Sheringham Hall.

Henry Ramey Upcher on the occasion of his golden wedding anniversary in 1888, at which 1,000 guests were entertained at a party at Sheringham Hall.

that when she returned to Woburn she wrote to Thomas making an offer to buy both. When Thomas met the Duke at a cocktail party in London he told the story to the Duke, who expressed an interest in seeing Sheringham Hall and estate. He and his wife then spent a weekend as guests of Thomas and a lasting friendship was formed.

Other suggestions made by Repton were to remove the wall around the workhouse building, to provide a maypole, to allow parishioners free access to the woodlands to remove fallen branches and other wood and to bring back the sport of coursing, previously held regularly on the beach. All these would, in Repton's opinion, improve the relationship between the parishioners and the squire.

Henry Ramey married Caroline Morris on 3 June 1838. They had four sons and a daughter and were the first occupiers of Sheringham Hall, the rooms of which were furnished properly for the first time, especially the living-room, which ran along the eastern elevation of the building. His mother, Charlotte, moved into the Old Farm House, where she lived until her death in 1857. In 1838 her father had inherited the title of Lord Berners and from then on she had been known as 'The Honourable' by her servants and most of the people who benefited from her generous and charitable nature.

Henry Ramey continued the philanthropic activi-

Henry Ramey and Caroline Upcher in later life. He was Sheringham's local squire for 73 years.

152

ties established by his parents, including his mother's active support of the anti-slavery movement. He was a good all-round sportsman, especially as a cricketer.

He did not share his father's love of coursing, although he, like his brother Abbot, did become an ardent sportsman, particularly with tuition from Larry Banville, gamekeeper to Sir Thomas Fowell Buxton, with whom they often went hunting. On Monday 7, September 1829, he went shooting with Abbot and Arthur, recording in his diary that they:

'... were nice young gentlemen, but I must say that Abbot is as wild as any young willock (guillemot) *that e'er was on the sea coast, but a good natured young man.*

Henry Ramey died on 30 March 1892 'at the ripe age of 82'. The mourners represented the cream of Norfolk society, and those who could not attend, such as Mr R.H.J. Gurney and Mr J.B. Firth of Barningham Hall, sent their carriages. Henry was remembered as an active Deputy Lord Lieutenant of the county and as a squire always willing to help the poor in both Upper and Lower Sheringham, particularly the members of the fishing community, when times were hard. He had been a committed member of the Liberal Party and brought his liberal views to his appointment as chairman of the local bench of magistrates, where 'many a prisoner has had occasion to thank him for a lenient sentence'. His hospitality was well known, with such national figures as Lord Tennyson, Charles Dickens and Sir John Tenniel received as guests at Sheringham Hall.

Henry Morris Upcher was born on 15 December 1839, becoming the local squire and developing into an all-round sportsman, a keen naturalist and a local benefactor. He is remembered 'as a shooter of game with few equals', specialising in the shooting of woodcock, of which he probably brought down over 100 every season.

Prior to inheriting the Sheringham estate in 1892 he accompanied two naturalist friends on an expedition to Iceland, then, in 1863, took part in expeditions to Palestine, the Dead Sea and the Sea of Galilee. Whilst in Palestine scantily dressed women from a nearby village came to dance for the visitors. It was recorded that 'the Englishmen were not impressed', Henry being more interested in a jungle cat caught in one of his traps.

A wildfowling journal kept by William Bolding Monement highlights some of the 'sporting' activities undertaken by members of the Upcher family:

11 October 1881 – A punting trip to Holland with Hammy Upcher Sailed from Harwich 13 October – 12 November. 596 fowl in 27 days.
9 October 1882 – A shooting trip to Duckland with Hammy. Harwich to Rotterdam 11–25 October. 233 fowl in 13 days.
10 February 1883 – A shooting trip to Fairlie, Scotland, with Edward Upcher. Left Lynn. 12–18 Feb. 35 in six days.
21 October 1886 – Wildfowling in Holland with Hamilton Upcher. Left Holt 23 Oct–3 Nov. 170 fowl in 10 days.
18 October 1888 – Left Cromer 20 Oct–3 Nov. (No destination given.) *102 fowl in 10 days.*

It was recorded that the sale of the birds at Leadenhall Market often paid for the expense of these trips, until the authorities increased the cost of the required licence.

Arthur Hamilton Upcher, son of Henry Ramey and known as 'Hammy' to his family and friends, is remembered for a variety of reasons. He was credited with being one of the best game shots in the country, was the first captain of Sheringham Golf Club and in his fishing activities caught the heaviest sea trout (21lbs) known at that time; it was a superb specimen, caught in the Bothy Pool on the River Awe a few miles inland from Oban. The fish is now on display in the Sheringham Museum. He served in the Royal Navy for a short period, leaving to take Holy Orders and eventually becoming rector of Baconsthorpe before retiring to Holt, where he was appointed a canon and chaplain to the Kelling Tuberculosis Sanitorium. He is also remembered as never taking a proper bath, preferring to use a hipbath in front of a bedroom fire. His preferred relaxation was to read the *Daily Mail* and cowboy books taken out of the Holt library. He established a bowls club on the lawn at the back of his house, 'Shrublands', close to Holt Station, but his overriding passion, apparently, was watching any match involving the Holt football team. He died in Holt at the age of 80.

Henry Morris, son of Henry Ramey, like his brothers, acquired a reputation as a sportsman, with cricket his main interest. He was a renowned naturalist, a fellow of the Zoological Society and much in demand as a speaker on all aspects of bird life. His charitable works included donating the land for the former recreation ground in Holt Road, contributing to the cost of the war memorial and providing financial support for the upkeep of the *Augusta* lifeboat.

Henry Sparke Upcher, son of Henry Morris, inherited the Sheringham estate in 1920. Like his predecessors, he involved himself in local affairs, supporting the local branch of the Royal Society for the Protection of Birds, the Rivers Board and the Norfolk and Norwich Naturalists' Society. He was the third member of the Upcher family to be appointed President of the Golf Club, this being followed by the chairmanship of both the County War Agriculture Executive Committee and the Norfolk County Council.

Abbot married Mary Jones Day and became

A photograph taken at St Andrew's, St Joseph's Road, Sheringham, in October 1926. Left to right: Miss Sybil Upcher, Canon Arthur Upcher, Miss Mary Upcher, Margaret Upcher (wife of Canon Arthur Upcher), Hilda Upcher, Archdeacon Haye Upcher. Note the absence of buildings beyond this property which, at the time of writing is the Whitehaven residential home.

Arthur Wilson Upcher with his daughters, Emma Mary and Jane Charlotte.

Sheringham Hall dairy milk float with, left to right, William Cooper, Mr Hancock, William Slater Loades.

curate at Flixton, just south of Bungay in Suffolk, then rector of Kirby Cane in Norfolk until his death in 1889. Arthur Wilson Upcher is remembered largely for the fact that he rowed No. 7 in the Cambridge boat in the first boat race, held in 1836. His crew beat the Oxford boat by one minute. On leaving college he took the curacy of Hughenden in Buckinghamshire, followed by a similar position at Upper Sheringham before becoming, finally, rector of Ashwellthorpe and Wreningham. Whilst the family could celebrate Arthur's success in the boat race, they were to face a sad bereavement when Charlotte's youngest daughter, Augusta, died of tuberculosis on 15 September 1836 at the early age of 26. She was buried on 21 September, local carpenter Richard Sunman acting as funeral director and with local men as coffin bearers and pallbearers. Among the former were Ottey, Wegg, T. Cooper, Nunn, W. Pegg, 'Cutler' Craske, Harry Grice and Robert Bishop. The pallbearers included Barcham, L. Lown, Long, Clerk, Pigott, London and Cranefield. Pupils from Upper Sheringham school followed behind the hearse.

Just two months later, on 29 November, Sheringham was hit by a 'dreadful' storm, Emma Pigott recording that eight local men were swept out to sea and drowned whilst fishing for crabs near to the shore. She lists them as Cutler Craske and his son Nat; old William Little, John Wilson, Loads Bishop and his two sons, aged 22 and 16, and Paul Bishop's son, aged 22.

By now Sheringham had allotments in full use, the first having been provided by Charlotte Upcher in September 1831. She let six acres of land in ten

Sir Henry Edward Sparke Upcher, father of Henry Thomas Simpson Upcher, in 1954. He received his knighthood in 1942.

During the 1946 Royal Norfolk Show, Sir Henry Upcher, in his role as Chairman of the Norfolk Agricultural Executive Committee, has the pleasant duty of congratulating 21 Women's Land Army girls on their six years in the service. The proceedings are watched by Dowager Lady Suffield, Chairman of the Norfolk WLA committee.

Henry Thomas Simpson Upcher. It was his wish that the Sheringham Hall Estate be taken over by the National Trust.

half-acre lots and a further four quarter-acre lots to Nunn, Wegg, Risbro, Moy, Loads, John Smith, L. Howell, Steward, Chapman, Shepherd and John Cooper. The latter had a half acre at £1 per annum and a further quarter acre at 10s. a year. It was a condition of tenure that all allotments be cultivated 'with spade husbandry', and that each gardener preserve the fence 'opposite his own garden'.

The diary of Arthur Wilson Upcher records his successful attempt to build a Chapel of Ease in Lower Sheringham, the town, at that time, having no church. Initially he considered buying and converting an old fish house. Encouraged by support from the Bishop of Norwich, Arthur changed his mind and bought a piece of garden owned by local man Robert Cooper. Building started in August 1841, with two local farmers offering the services, free of any charge, of their horses and wagons to cart materials such as flints to the building site.

On Sunday, 31 October the same year, Arthur was told by Cooper that the townspeople 'were rejoycing' that they would soon have their own Chapel of Ease. Arthur, however, was a bit cautious, recording that he thought the main reason for this was '... now they will not have to pay for seats as they have at the Methodist Chapel. The chapel was opened on Sunday, 23 January 1842, with Arthur, in his role as curate of Sheringham, giving the sermon, taking as

his text the words: 'Who commanded you to build chis house and to make these walls?' from the Book of Ezra.

The night before the opening there had been an exceptional fall of snow, resulting in the party from Sheringham Hall travelling to Lower Sheringham in a sledge. Despite the bad weather every seat was occupied. A new Sunday school started on 14 March 1842 with 40 children attending. The planned mixture of boys from both Upper and Lower Sheringham 'caused them to run riot', and they were 'turned out' a quarter of an hour before the service started. Arthur died on 11 June 1896.

The site of the Chapel of Ease was on land occupied in 2009 by a block of flats known as Temple Court, just off Morris Street.

The last of the Upcher family to live in Sheringham Hall was Henry Thomas Simpson Upcher, who took over the estate in 1954 after living for many years abroad. It is to him that we owe the present development of the grounds, with their walks and magnificent display of varieties of rhododendrons, which attract thousands of visitors during the spring and summer months. He was the last of the Upcher men to be president of the Golf Club. He was very much a family man and the hall once again became a social centre for family and friends. Towards the end of his life, in 1985, he expressed his wish that the hall should be taken over by the National Trust. About a year later, in November 1986, the latter completed negotiations for the purchase of the park and hall, including the family portraits and the contents of the living-room.

The sale of furniture, pictures, ceramics and silver, the property of the Trustees of Henry Thomas's estate, took place on Wednesday and Thursday, 22–23 October 1986. The auctioneers were Christie, Manson & Woods Ltd of London and the company's director, Henry Wyndham, conducted the auction, which was held in a large marquee erected in the hall grounds. In addition to 'the London trade' there were dealers and individual bidders from around the world. By the end of the first day well over £1 million had been taken, strong interest being focused on the collection of Regency furniture and the paintings by Dutch Masters, £100,000 being paid for a still life by Paul Theodor van Brussel, signed and dated 1790. The Trustees, obviously, were pleased with the successful outcome of the sale. Their chairman, Mr Maurice Heath, confirmed it had gone 'extremely well', adding: 'Almost everything fetched what we expected and more, and very few went for figures lower than we anticipated.'

The National Trust has let Sheringham Hall to family tenants and it is not open to the public. The majority of the 800 acres of parkland is open to the public and provides pleasant walks with superb countryside and sea views, making Sheringham Park one of the town's top tourist attractions.

Sheringham Through the Years

The Olley family's coaches, Lifeboat Plain, c.1880. In the background is the Lifeboat House, with stairs up to the Fishermen's Reading Room.

C.T. Baker bought these premises in the High Street from the Upcher estate in about 1888, and in 1896 they were valued at £900. The 1900 premises were described as 'an ironmongery shop and two empty cottages, adjoining workshop and stable at the back'. Customers have recalled the wide variety of goods sold, so many, in fact, that the aisles were so narrow you had to walk sideways up and down them! C.T. Baker moved out of the shop in 1954, the site being sold to Woolworth's, who occupied it until all their stores were closed in the spring of 2009.

Sheringham Through the Years

Barnes's toyshop in the High Street was destroyed by fire in 1906.

The Cooperative Bakery on the corner of Cremer Street and Cooperative Street.

Subscribers

Derek and Megan Baldry, Sheringham
Joyce and Ruth Batchelor, Sheringham, Norfolk
The Baxter Family, Sheringham
Rosemary and David Bishop, Sheffield, South Yorkshire
Sally Boucherat, Norwich
Sue and Tony Bourne, Sheringham, Norfolk
Benjiman Johnson Brown (Toosh), Sheringham
Mr and Mrs F. T. H. Bullock and Family, Sheringham, Norfolk
Phil and Claire Busby, Sheringham
Mr Alan Chastney, Sheringham, Norfolk
Michael J. Childs, Sheringham, Norfolk
David Clayton, Sheringham, Norfolk
Mrs Yvonne Constable (née Craske)
Roy S. Craske, Redbourn, Herts
Hazel Craske, Sheringham
Mr Nigel A. Cumming, Sheringham
Roslyn Cummins, Sheringham
Alan Davies, Sheringham, Norfolk
Ann A. Dennis, Weymouth, Dorset
Sue Dockray (née James), Sheringham born
Jack Ecroyd, Sheringham
Mrs Diana Ecroyd, Sheringham
Francis J. L. Farrow, Sheringham, Norfolk
Arthur Fincham, Sheringham
Keith Forsdick, Heanor, Derbyshire
Brian T. Fountain, Sheringham, Norfolk
Drs J. and M. Gardiner, Sheringham
Chris and Dulcia Gardner
Maxwell J. Garrett
Alan and Margaret Gibling, Sheringham
Cherry Gibson, Springfield, Kentucky
Paul and Pam Girardot, Sheringham
Ray and Lucille Grand, Sheringham, Norfolk
Ian Grimes,
Leslie and Margery Grimes, Sheringham, Norfolk
Dorothy and Alec Hancock, Sheringham, Norfolk
Jacqueline F. Harris, Sheringham, Norfolk
The Hart Family, Sheringham
Hastings' Fruiterers, Sheringham, Norfolk
Michael Hill, Sheringham
Jacqueline Isted (née Gray)
Peter Alec Jeary, Born Co-op Street, Sheringham
M. Knowles, Beeston Common, Sheringham
Margaret and Roy Lemon, Sheringham
D. J. and J. C. Litchfield, Sheringham, Norfolk
Mr Douglas J. Macgregor, Sheringham, Norfolk
George Mann, Sheringham
Kevin Mann, Romford & Richard Mann, Llanelli,
Georgina Martin, Seaview, Sheringham
Heather J. Matthews, Beeston Regis
Richard and Penny May, Sheringham
Derek and Val McCall, Creswell, Derbyshire
Dr David Mellor, West Bridgford, Nottingham

Marion E. Middleton, Sherborne, Dorset
Kay and David Moore, Duffield, Derbys
Annette Moore (née Farrow), Blackpool, Lancs
Ian Morter, Derby
John Mutimer, Hitchin, Herts
Barrie D. Mutimer, Walsoken, Norfolk
Mrs Janet E. Newman, Chatham, Kent
Mr Peter L. Newman, Chatham, Kent
Sue and Ken Norman, Sheringham
Martin B. Olley
Geoffrey Paice, Sheringham, Norfolk
Dennis S. Papworth OBE, Sheringham
John M. G. Payne, Beeston Regis, Sheringham
Dr David Pickersgill, Sheringham, Norfolk
Les Pigott, Sheringham
Michael Pike, Sheringham
Mr and Mrs Paul John Pretty, Sheringham, Norfolk
Elsie M. Radley, Upper Sheringham, Norfolk
Wendy M. Rawlings
P. F. and D. E. Richmond, Sheringham, Norfolk
John Sadler, Sheringham
Mr G. Scothern, Sheffield
Michael and Pauline Slipper (née Childs), Sheringham, Norfolk
Edward Smith, Sheringham, Norfolk
Marilyn Sparkes, Crowthorne, Berks
Peggy Stratton, Sheringham
Mrs Peggy Strudwick, Sheringham
Charles and Jan Thirtle, Sheringham
Barbara J. Thirtle, Sheringham
Peter Tissier, Seaview, Sheringham
Mr R. and Mrs S. D. Toyn, Sheringham, Norfolk
Mrs Diana Trant, Bishops Stortford, Herts
Miriam and Derek Welch, Sheringham, Norfolk
M. D. Wells, Common Lane, Sheringham
Peter John West, Beeston Regis, Norfolk
Robin and Linda West, Chapel-en-le-Frith, High Peak
B. C. H. and H. E. West, Sheringham
Paul and Betty Whitehouse, Sheringham
Catherine E. Wilson, Guelph, Ontario
Ms Marilyn Z. Woodrow
Kim and Ross Wordie, Sheringham
Maisie Wright
Mr Ronald Wright, Sheringham, Norfolk
Jack and Thelma Yates, Sheringham, Norfolk